A Simple German Handbook

with Graded Exercises

Peter Mann

Head of Languages, Yarborough High School, Lincoln

Edward Arnold

© Peter Mann 1979

First published 1979 by
Edward Arnold (Publishers) Ltd
41 Bedford Square, London WC1B 3DQ

Edward Arnold (Pty) Ltd
80 Waverley Road, Caulfield East
Victoria 3145, Australia

Reprinted 1981, 1984

British Library Cataloguing in Publication Data

Mann, Peter
    A simple German handbook with graded exercises.
    1. German language — Grammar — 1950-
    I. Title
    438' 2'421 PF 3112

ISBN 0-7131-0135-0

Set in 11 pt. Century by ⏀ Tek-Art, Croydon, Surrey, and printed in
Great Britain at The Pitman Press, Bath

Foreword

A Simple German Handbook with graded exercises is designed to help those who need a handy aid towards speaking and writing good accurate German and owes its title to two ideas which the author has in his approach to German grammar. The first is that the points should be simple, both in layout and in explanation. A knowledge of basic grammatical terminology is generally accepted by modern language teachers as indispensable to rapid language learning and the simplified 'grammar for linguists' section goes some way towards meeting this need.

The second idea is that a simple German grammar should be 'usable' in the fullest sense of the word. The points of grammar are clearly laid out, often in simplified box or table form, and clear explanations with examples accompany each one. After the point has been explained and demonstrated, the user has the chance to practise it by doing the exercises which follow. It is here that the book becomes a usable handbook, both for the learner and for the student revising.

The contents do not purport to be an exhaustive German reference — there are excellent examples of these already in print — but they represent an irreducible minimum of German grammar which will serve all students of first-level examinations, whatever course they may be using to learn the language.

Acknowledgements

A special debt of gratitude is owed to Michael Wild for his help and encouragement, particularly in the earlier stages; my thanks also to Fräulein Ilse Mechtersheimer of Neustadt-Lachen and Herr Roland Wingerter of Neustadt-Gimmeldingen for their assistance with script checking; and finally not least to my wife Elizabeth for her helpful suggestions and patience in typing of my manuscripts.

Peter Mann

Contents

Part I

Introduction to basic grammar in English

1 Parts of Speech

Nouns

Ideas, names of objects, living things and places are nouns.
E.g.: table; postman; mouse; light; courage; experience;
strength.

Articles

Definite article = the
Indefinite article (i.e. no particular one) = a; an

Adjectives

This is the name given to a word which describes a noun. E.g.:
a large table; an old house; the falling rain; the new orange light;
the broken glass; coffee is expensive.

Pronouns

These are words used in place of nouns.
> It instead of 'the house', or 'the sea', or 'my book'
> He instead of 'Mr McIntyre' or 'the boy'
> She instead of 'Marguerite' or 'the girl'
> We instead of 'my wife and I'

E.g.: The house is old and it has small windows
E.g.: Also they; him; I; me; you; us; who; which etc. are all
pronouns.

1

Verbs

The verb shows action or a state of being in a sentence, and often comes near the beginning. With it there is a noun (or pronoun) called the subject, which shows 'who' or 'what' does the action indicated by the verb. 'Who' does the action causes the form of the verb to vary.

> I run to school every day.
> The boy runs to school every day.
> We never run across roads.

'I', 'the boy' and 'we' are the subjects of these three sentences.

Objects

Objects are the nouns or pronouns which the verb acts on or affects. In English, they are mentioned after the verb.

> I saw the boy.
> We sold the car.

There are two types of object — direct and indirect. The above examples are direct objects.

> I showed the boy my photos.
> We bought him the present.

The above examples are indirect objects. An indirect object usually has the word 'to' or 'for' before the noun or pronoun. Sometimes, however, the 'to' or 'for' is left out, as it has been above. If you changed the word order slightly, though, you would see the 'to' or 'for':

> I showed my photos to the boy.
> We bought the present for him.

Prepositions

Words which show where someone/something is going or the position where someone/something is. E.g.: out of/to the house; at home; over/under the sea; in/into the drawer.
Prepositions are also met in other phrases: with/without me; for his brother.

Adverbs

Adverbs describe when/where/how things happen, e.g.: always; downstairs; quickly.

> My friend and I always run to school.
> He came downstairs quickly.

Adverbs also qualify an adjective or another adverb.
> He was surprisingly punctual.
> It is very hot.
> He did it extremely well.

In English adverbs often end in '-ly'.

Conjunctions

Conjunctions are joining words, e.g.: and; when.
> He came to see me and stayed for the weekend.
> When he came home, he was wet through.

All these parts of speech combine to form sentences.

2 The Sentence

The simplest possible sentence contains only one subject and one verb. E.g.: I slept. The doorbell rang. Some boys entered.

Notice that the subject is a noun or pronoun, showing who/ what did the action (the verb). This is a simple sentence:
> The boy stayed at home with his parents.

Simple because there is only one subject and one verb.

This sentence is made up of two simple sentences joined by a conjunction:
> The boy (subject) stayed (verb) at home with his parents because he (subject) had been (verb) ill.

How to break a sentence down into its main parts
> The boy gave his hat to his friend.

To find the verb: ask the question: What did the boy do? Answer = gave, so gave is the verb.

To find the subject: ask the question: Who/what does the action? The answer is the subject of the sentence, and is a noun or pronoun. Answer = the boy, so this is the subject.

To find the direct object: ask the question: whom/what did the boy give? The answer is always a noun or pronoun. Here it is his hat which is the direct object.

To find the indirect object: ask the question: to whom/to what did the boy give his hat? The answer is the indirect object, again either a noun or pronoun. Here it is to his friend.

3 Verb Tenses

Actions can be in the past, present or future. Here is the English verb 'to go' written out in these three tenses:

Past

I went/did go/have gone/
    was going
you went/did go/have gone
    were going
he ⎱
she ⎱ went/did go/
it   ⎰ has gone/was
the boy ⎰ going

we went/did go/have gone/
    were going
you went/did go/have gone/
    were going
they went/did go/have gone/
    were going
the boys went/did go/have gone/
    were going
Andy and John went/did go/
    have gone/were going

Present

I go/am going
you go/are going
he ⎱
she ⎱
it   ⎰ goes/is going
the boy ⎰

we go/are going
you go/are going
they go/are going
the boys go/are going
Andy and John go/are going

Future

I shall go/shall be going
you will go/will be going
he ⎱
she ⎱ will go/will be
it   ⎰ going
the boy ⎰

we shall go/shall be going
you will go/will be going
they will go/will be going
the boys will go/will be going
Andy and John will go/will be
    going

Note that the continuous forms (ending in '-ing') in all tenses are expressed in German by the one form:
    ich gehe means 'I go' or 'I am going'.
    ich werde gehen means 'I shall go' or 'I shall be going'.

4

The tense of the verb is often shown in advance by a time expression:

Past expressions	Present	Future
yesterday	today	tomorrow (morning)
last year/week	at the moment	next week/ year etc.
(some time) ago	at present	in ten years'/ days' time

4 Number and Gender

Number

Singular and plural are the two terms which show number.

Singular

One chair; the chair; a chair; this/that chair — all these mean one single chair, so the words one; the; a; this/that and chair are all singular.

Plural

Some chairs; many chairs; the chairs; these/those chairs — all these expressions mean more than one chair. The words some; many; the; these/those and chairs are all plural.

Words like I; he; it; you are all singular (mean one person). We; you and they are plural (mean more than one person).

Gender

In English, gender means masculine or feminine. In German, however, there are three genders: masculine, neuter and feminine. Things in English (e.g. book; chair) are neuter, being neither masculine nor feminine. In the German language all things have a gender, either masculine, neuter or feminine. A table happens to be masculine, a book neuter, a lamp feminine. There is no simple reason for this; it just has to be learned as such.

Part II

1 Introduction to case

As you have seen in the introductory grammar section to this book, nouns and pronouns can do several jobs. They can be a subject, direct object or indirect object. In German, the article (a, an, the) which precedes the noun, changes according to the job the noun is doing. There are four cases, in German:

The **Nominative** Case — *der* — acts as subject.
The **Accusative** Case — *den* — acts as direct object.
The **Dative** Case — *dem* — acts as indirect object.
The **Genitive** Case — *des* — acts as an object of a preposition or shows ownership.

Note: *der, den, dem, des* above are the masculine singular forms.

The nominative case

All nouns in German are shown in dictionaries and vocabulary lists in the nominative case, e.g. you look up table in a dictionary and you find *der Tisch*; book — *das Buch*; lamp — *die Lampe*.

Der, das and *die* (masculine, neuter and feminine respectively) are the three German equivalents for the in English. (Words that use *der* and *das* use *ein* to say a or an. *Die* words use *eine*.) You can only know which of the three fits a particular noun by looking the noun up in a dictionary or vocabulary.

Form of the Articles with a Subject Noun

the	der	Mann	
a	ein	Mann	
the	das	Buch	will be shown in future in the shorter forms:
a	ein	Buch	
the	die	Lampe	
a	eine	Lampe	

der/ein Mann
das/ein Buch
die/eine Lampe

The plural form in the nominative case is always *die*.

Usage

The nominative is the subject case. Words which form the subject of a sentence are in this case. As there are three genders in the singular, there are three forms of the nominative case.

Masculine: *Der Mann* (subject) kommt (verb) spät.
Neuter: *Das Buch* (subject) liegt (verb) auf dem Tisch.
Feminine: *Die Lampe* (subject) fällt (verb) zu Boden.

For the *ein* word forms, see above.

Note 1   *der, das* and *die* are also used after the verbs *sein*, to be, *werden*, to become, and *bleiben*, to remain.

Sein Vater ist *der* reichste Mann in Landau.
Er wurde *ein* fleißiger Student.
In den folgenden Jahren blieb Köln *eine* interessante Stadt.

Note 2   Nominative adjective ending (singular): if an adjective is used after *der, das,* and *die* or *ein* and *eine*, it must take an ending, as shown in the following table:

der	-e	ein	-er	Er ist ein gut*er* Mann.
das	-e	ein	-es	Ein schön*es* Haus kostet viel Geld.
die	-e	eine	-e	Sie ist eine fleißig*e* Hausfrau.

7

Note 3 Nominative adjective ending (plural): there is of course no plural of *ein*, and words like *mein* (see p. 23), when followed by an adjective in the plural, use the same adjective endings as the definite article. *Der, das* and *die* all go to the same form *die* in the plural and add the following endings:

die	-en	*Die* schöns*ten* Kleider sind nicht billig.
meine	-en	*Meine* beid*en* Brüder sind hier.

Exercises

A

Supply the correct form of the definite/indefinite article, and copy the sentence.

1   D____ Land ist sehr schön.
2   D____ Sparkassenleiter ist Herr Schmidt.
3   Ei ____ Zeitung kostet nur 50 Pf.
4   Hier ist ei____ Bleistift, Roland.
5   Wo ist d____ Buch?

Continue, supplying an adjective ending wherever necessary as well.

6   D____ nett____ Onkel wohnt hier.
7   Wo ist d____ neu____ Lampe?
8   Ei____ begabt____ Ingenieur entwarf jene Brücke.
9   Ei____ unartig____ Kind macht viel Lärm.
10   Helmut ist kei____ fleißig____ Schüler.
11   Sie möchte ei____ berühmt____ Tänzerin werden.
12   Wo sind d____ neu____ Bücher?
13   All____ gut____ Dinge sind drei.
14   Sie ist ei____ nett____ Mädchen.
15   D____ alt____ Haus steht in der Bahnhofstraße.

B

Using the vocabulary given in the box at the end of this exercise, translate the English phrases into German, and copy out the whole sentence.

1   The bad-tempered postman/stieß unseren Hund mit dem Fuß.
2   Wo sind/the new tennis shoes/, die ich gestern kaufte?

3 Das war/a funny play.
4 The modern hotel/brannte nieder.
5 The angry teacher/kam ins Klassenzimmer.
6 A black cat/lief ins Haus.
7 The smaller children/essen gern Eis.
8 Er ist/a very clever boy.
9 Sie wurde/the richest lady/in der Stadt.
10 The hungry soldiers/aßen einen ganzen Ochsen auf.

Nouns

Masculine (der)	*Neuter* (das)	*Feminine* (die)
Briefträger	Schauspiel	Lehrerin
Tennisschuh (—e)	Hotel	Katze
Junge	Kind (—er)	Dame
Soldat (—en)		

Adjectives

schlechtgelaunt, neu, komisch, modern, böse, schwarz, kleiner, klug, hungrig, (der, das, die) reichste.

The accusative case

Form

In the accusative case, only the masculine singular changes.

| der/ein words ⟶ *den/einen* |
| das/ein ⎫ |
| die/eine ⎭ words ⟶ remain unchanged |

Nominative form		*Accusative form*	
		the	*a, an*
der Tisch (table) ⟶		*den* Tisch	*einen* Tisch
das Buch (book) ⟶		*das* Buch	*ein* Buch
die Zeitung (newspaper) ⟶		*die* Zeitung	*eine* Zeitung

9

Note: the adjective ending after *den/einen* is *—en*.
Wir gingen durch den/einen groß*en* Wald.
The adjective ending after *das* remains *—e*.
after *ein* (neuter) remains *—es*.
after *die/eine* remains *—e*.
In the plural form, the adjective after *die* ends in *—en*.

Usage

The accusative case is used in the following ways:
a) for the direct object (see English grammar notes, p. 2);
b) after prepositions which always take the accusative;
c) with phrases of motion after mixed prepositions;
d) in expressions of definite time, e.g. letzten Dienstag (last Tuesday);
e) duration of time, e.g. den ganzen Tag (all day long).

a) **Direct object**

Examples:
Ich (*subject*) **kaufe** (*verb*) **den Tisch** (*direct object*) **zu DM 600.**
(I'm buying the table for 600 marks.)

Wir (*subject*) **kennen** (*verb*) **einen sehr freundlichen Arbeiter** (*direct object).*
(We know a very friendly workman.)

Den Mann (*direct object*) **kennt** (*verb*) **der Polizist** (*subject*) **nicht.**
(The policeman doesn't know that man.)

b) **Prepositions that always take the accusative case**

durch	— through	*ohne*	— without
für	— for	*um*	— round, at
gegen	— against	*wider*	— contrary to (opinion etc.)
bis	— until	*entlang*	— along (follows its noun)

Examples:
Sie gingen *durch den Wald.* (der Wald)
(They walked through the wood.)

10

Die zwei Brüder kamen *um die Ecke.* (die Ecke)
(The two brothers came round the corner.)

Er kam *ohne das Buch.* (das Buch)
(He came without the book.)

Sie fuhr *die Hauptstraße entlang.* (die Hauptstraße)
(She drove along the High Street.)

Bis nächsten Montag. (der Tag)
(Until next Monday.)

Note: The accusative case is *always* used with these prepositions. Note also the special use of *gegen* and *um*:

gegen vier Uhr	(about four o'clock, getting on for four o'clock)
um vier Uhr	(at four o'clock)

c) Phrases of Motion after Mixed Prepositions

When the verb suggests motion towards (e.g. *gehen, laufen, rollen* and, not so obviously, *legen, stellen* and *klopfen*), and one of the prepositions in the following list is used, then the accusative case must be used.

Remember: accusative for motion. (See also the notes on the dative case, p. 18).

in	—	into	*hinter*	—	behind
an	—	onto*	*neben*	—	near, beside
auf	—	onto**	*vor*	—	in front of
unter	—	under	*zwischen*	—	between
über	—	over			

*used with vertical or sloping surfaces
**used with horizontal surfaces

Er *lief in das Zimmer.* (das Zimmer)
(He ran into the room.)

Ich *klopfte an die Tür.* (die Tür)
(I knocked on the door.)

Ich *legte* das Buch *auf den Tisch.* (der Tisch)
(I put the book on the table.)

Der Ball *rollte unter den Stuhl.* (der Stuhl)
(The ball rolled under the chair.)

Der Vogel *flog über den Garten.* (der Garten)
(The bird flew over the garden.)

Exercises

A

Supply the necessary missing endings, and copy each sentence.

Direct object

1 Ich nehme ei___ Regenschirm mit. (der Regenschirm)
2 D___ Hemd kaufe ich. (das Hemd)
3 Liest du jeden Abend ei___Buch? (das Buch)
4 Haben Sie d___Zeitung von gestern? (die Zeitung)
5 Hier kauft man ei___Fahrkarte. (die Fahrkarte)

Accusative prepositions

6 Er ging, ohne ei___Wort zu sagen. (das Wort)
7 Wir gingen durch d___Wald. (der Wald)
8 Das Mädchen lief um ei___Baum herum. (der Baum)
9 Ich mache es für ei___ Freund. (der Freund)
10 Er stellte sein Rad gegen ei___ Mauer. (die Mauer)

Phrases of motion

11 Wir liefen in d___Park. (der Park)
12 Sie legte den Mantel auf ei___ Stuhl. (der Stuhl)
13 Der Mann klopfte an d___Tür. (die Tür)
14 Die Katze sprang hinter d___Vorhang. (der Vorhang)
15 Er stellte sich unter d___Dusche. (die Dusche)

B

Copy the following, filling in the missing endings.
1 Ich sah d___alt___ Dame, wie sie in d___ Park ging.
(die Dame; der Park)
2 Der junge Mann nahm d___ schwer___ Koffer [singular]
vom Gepäcknetz herunter. (der Koffer)

3   Alle Ehepaare möchten ei__ eigen__ Wohnung. (die Wohnung)
4   Das Kind machte sich d__ Schuhe sehr schmutzig. (der Schuh)
5   Er kauft nur d __ letzt __ Ausgaben. (die Ausgabe)
6   Das Kind aß ei__ knusprig __Keks. (der Keks)
7   Wir machten ei__ lang__ermüdend__ Ausflug. (der Ausflug)
8   Ich holte d__ best__Weingläser aus dem Schrank. (das Weinglas)
9   Wir sahen d__ alt__Haus einstürzen. (das Haus)
10 Herr Winkler schenkte dem klügsten Jungen ei__ sehr interessant__Buch. (das Buch)

The genitive case

This is used to show possession or ownership, and can often be avoided by using 'von' with the dative case.

Form

Singular	der/ein	des/eines	(−s or −es added to the noun)
	das/ein		
	die/eine	der/einer	(no change to the feminine noun)
Plural	die	der	(no change to the plural noun)

Note: in the genitive case, singular and plural, the adjective always ends in −en.
Das ist das Haus eines guten Freundes.
(That is the house of a good friend.)

Sie ist im Büro der jungen Sekretärin.
(She is in the young secretary's office.)

13

Usage

a) To denote ownership or possession, where English uses
—'s or,—s', e.g. The boy's house (house of the boy);
the workers' club (the club of the workers).
See above for German examples.

b) After prepositions which always take the genitive (usually
including the word 'of' in English).

trotz	—	in spite of
wegen	—	because of
außerhalb	—	outside (the town etc.)
innerhalb	—	inside (the town etc.)
während	—	during
(an) statt	—	instead of

Trotz des schlechten Wetters kam er. (das Wetter)
(He came in spite of the bad weather.)

Wegen der Kälte frieren wir. (die Kälte)
(We are freezing because of the cold)

Wir wohnen *außerhalb der Stadt.* (die Stadt)
(We live outside the town.)

Er wohnt *innerhalb des Dorfes.* (das Dorf)
(He lives in the village.)

Während der Ferien machen wir nichts. (die Ferien, plural)
(During the holidays we don't do anything.)

Statt eines Briefes schrieb er eine Postkarte. (der Brief)
(He wrote a postcard instead of a letter.)

Exercises

A

Copy the following, filling in the blanks.
1 Die Ursache d___Krieg___ ist noch unbekannt. (der Krieg)
2 Der Hut d___Frau ist zu groß für sie. (die Frau)
3 Das Dach d___ Haus___war eingefallen. (das Haus)
4 Das sind die Schuhe ei___Dame. (die Dame)
5 Ich höre die Stimmen d___Kinder. (das Kind)

14

Using the words given, translate the following phrases into German.

6 At the end of the street (am Ende; die Straße)
7 At the beginning of the year (am Anfang; das Jahr)
8 My father's mother (i.e. the mother of my father) (die Mutter; mein Vater)
9 The leaves of the trees (das Blatt, ⸚ er; der Baum, ⸚e)
10 The pocket of the coat (die Tasche; die Jacke)

B

Copy the following, translating the English portions of each sentence into German.

1 Wir machten unser Picknick/in spite of the bad weather. (das Wetter)
2 Wir besuchten/my rich uncle's old castle. (der Onkel; die Burg)
3 Ich nahm meinen Regenmantel/instead of my anorak. (der Anorak)
4 Der alte Mann ist/during the very interesting performance/ eingeschlafen. (die Vorstellung)
5 Because of the many diversions/kamen sie sehr spät im Büro an. (die Umleitung, —en)
6 The boys' father/schickte sie sofort ins Bett. (der Vater; der Junge, —n)
7 Inside the church/war uns sehr kalt. (die Kirche)
8 My mother's dog/ist in den Park gegangen. (der Hund; meine Mutter)
9 The head of a large comprehensive school/wird immer gut bezahlt. (der Direktor; die Gesamtschule)
10 Er tat es/within a month. (der Monat)

The dative case

The dative case is the case which means to or for, needing no extra words for these, e.g. *dem Mann* = to/for the man; *einer Frau* = to/for a woman. It is used in this way for the indirect object (see overleaf).

15

Form

der/ein words	}
das/ein words	} *dem/einem*
die/eine words	*der/einer*

Note: the adjective ending after *dem/einem, der/einer* is *—en*.
In the plural, *die* becomes *den*, and the adjective ending is *—en*.
The noun plural must also end in *—n* (if it does not do so
already), e.g. *den* meist*en* Leut*en* = to/for most people.

Usage

The dative case is used in the following ways:

a) for the indirect object (see English grammar notes, p. 2), the
    meaning being 'to' or 'for', without a preposition.
b) after those prepositions which always take the dative.
c) with phrases of position after mixed prepositions.
d) after certain verbs which take the dative case.

a) Indirect object

Er (subject) gab (verb) *dem Mann* (indirect object)
das Buch (direct object).
(He gave the book *to the man*.)
Vater (subject) reicht (verb) *dem Kind* (indirect object)
einen Spaten (direct object).
(Father handed (to) the child a spade.)

Note the order of the noun objects in the German:
indirect (i.e. dative) before direct (accusative). See also Note
3 on pronouns, p. 25.)

b) Prepositions that always take the Dative Case

mit	—	with	*aus*	—	out of
nach	—	after	*bei*	—	at (the house of)
von	—	from,	*seit*	—	since
		of			
zu	—	to	*gegenüber*	—	opposite
					(occasionally
					follows its noun)

Komme *mit deinem Bruder.* (der Bruder)
(Come with your brother.)

Er kommt *von meiner Schwester.* (die Schwester)
(He's come from my sister.)

Wir gehen *zur Schule.* (die Schule)
(We are going to school.)

Er kommt *aus dem Haus.* (das Haus)
(He is coming out of the house.)

Ich wohne *bei meinem Onkel.* (der Onkel)
(I live at my uncle's.)

Seit dem Krieg wohnen wir hier. (der Krieg)
(We've been living here since the war.)

Er wohnt *dem Bahnhof gegenüber.* (der Bahnhof)
(He lives opposite the station.)

Note also the special uses of these dative prepositions:

mit	mit dem Zug } mit der Bahn }	by train
	mit lauter Stimme	in a loud voice
nach	nach Hause	(towards) home
	nach Deutschland	to Germany
	nach Paris	to Paris
von	der König von England	the King of England
	ein Buch von Schiller	a book by Schiller
zu	zu Hause	at home
	zu Fuß	on foot
	zu Pferde	on horseback
	zu Weihnachten	at Christmas
	zu Ostern	at Easter
	zum Mittagessen	for dinner
aus	er kommt aus Berlin	he comes from Berlin
	aus Holz	made of wood
bei	bei schlechtem Wetter	in bad weather
	beim Fußballspielen	while playing football
seit	seit zwei Jahren	for the last two years

17

| gegenüber | einem gegenüber freundlich sein | to be friendly towards someone |

Note: *in dem, an dem, von dem, zu dem, bei dem* are usually shortened to *im, am, vom, zum, beim; zu der* shortens to *zur.*

c) **Phrases of Position after Mixed Prepositions**

When the verb suggests position (e.g. *sein, sitzen, liegen, sich befinden, stehen*) and one of the prepositions in the following list is used, then the dative case must be used. Remember: dative for position. (See also the notes on the accusative, p. 11).

in	—	in	*hinter*	—	behind
an	—	on*	*neben*	—	beside, next to
auf	—	on**	*vor*	—	in front of
unter	—	under	*zwischen*	—	between
über	—	over, above			

*used with vertical or sloping surfaces
**used with horizontal surfaces

Er *sitzt in dem Zimmer.* (das Zimmer)
(He is sitting in the room.)

Das Bild *hängt an der Wand.* (die Wand)
(The picture is hanging on the wall.)

Das Buch *liegt auf dem Tisch.* (der Tisch)
(The book is lying on the table.)

Der Ball *liegt unter dem Stuhl.* (der Stuhl)
(The ball is under the chair.)

Die Wolke *hängt über der Stadt.* (die Stadt)
(The cloud hangs over the town.)

Er *steht hinter dem Haus.* (das Haus)
(He is standing behind the house.)

Sie *stand vor der Klasse.* (die Klasse)
(She stood in front of the class.)

Er *stand zwischen den Bäumen.* (die Bäume, plural)
(He stood between the trees.)

18

d) Verbs which govern an object in the Dative Case.

glauben	— to believe	*helfen*	—	to help
danken	— to thank	*folgen*	—	to follow
wünschen	— to wish	*gelingen*	—	to succeed
gehören	— to belong to			

Er *half seiner Frau* bei ihrer Arbeit. (die Arbeit)
(He helped his wife with her work.)

Der Lehrer *glaubte dem Kind* nicht. (das Kind)
(The teacher did not believe the child.)

Das Buch *gehört meiner Tochter.* (die Tochter)
(The book belongs to my daughter.)

Exercises

A

Copy the following sentences, filling in the gaps.

Indirect object

1 Er gab ei___ Mann eine Zigarette. (der Mann)
2 Der Junge erzählte d___ Frau eine Geschichte. (die Frau)
3 Ich schenkte d___ Großvater eine Zigarre. (der Großvater)
4 Der Lehrer gab ei___ Kind das Klassenbuch. (das Kind)
5 Wir beschreiben ei___ Polizistin den Unfall. (die Polizistin)

Dative prepositions

6 Die Katze spielte mit ei___ Knäuel Wolle. (das Knäuel)
7 Nach d___ Essen tranken wir Kaffee. (das Essen)
8 Wir wohnen nicht weit von d___ See. (die See)
9 Die Touristen gingen zu ei___ Kirche. (die Kirche)
10 Er warf die Flasche aus ei___ Wagenfenster. (das Fenster)

Phrases of position

11 Meine Hose ist in d___ Kleiderschrank. (der Schrank)
12 Peter spielte an d___ Flußufer. (das Ufer)
13 Die Lampe stand auf ei___ Tisch. (der Tisch)
14 Die Katze lag hinter d___ Tür. (die Tür)
15 Der Direktor parkte vor ei___ Bäckerei. (die Bäckerei)

Verbs governing the dative

16 Der Polizist half ei___ Fräulein. (das Fräulein)
17 Er glaubte d___ Kind nicht. (das Kind)
18 Wir folgten d___ Stewardeß (die Stewardeß)
19 Sie dankte d___ Mann. (der Mann)
20 Sie wünschten d___ Direktor Frohe Weihnachten. (der Direktor)

B

Supply the correct form of the article and adjective endings.

Indirect object

1 Onkel Heinrich schenkte d___ brav___ Kind ein Buch zum Geburtstag.
2 Der Gymnasialdirektor schrieb d___ unzufrieden___ Mutter einen ausführlichen Brief.
3 Der Seemann warf ein___ ertrinkend___ Frau einen Rettungsring zu.
4 Der Millionär gab ein___ arm___ Landstreicher eine Zigarre.
5 Die Armut ist d___ meist___ jünger___ Leute___ unbekannt.

Dative prepositions

1 Jedes Auto ist mit ein___ modern___ Nebellampe ausgestattet.
2 Meine Mutter kaufte ihr Fleisch immer bei d___ freundlich___ Metzger.
3 Wein wird immer zu ei___ besonder___ Anlaß getrunken.
4 Nach d___ letzt___ Unruhen in Irland fahre ich nicht dorthin.
5 Der Preis wird von d___ ernst___ Finanzsituation der Welt beeinflußt.

Mixed prepositions and prepositional phrases

1 Die Kunden standen vor d___ geschlossen___ Ladentür.
2 Die Socken liegen unter d___ neu___ Hemden.
3 Ich möchte lieber auf ei___ riesig___ Passagierschiff sein.

4 Der Fußball lag hinter d___ gelb___Busch.
5 Der VW hielt an ei___ rot___Ampel.

Verbs with the dative

1 Der Priester glaubte d___ beichtend___Sünder.
2 Ich lief über die Straße, um ei___blind___Dame zu
   helfen.
3 Wir folgten d___ ausführlich___ Gebrauchsanweisungen
   sehr sorgfältig.
4 Herr Mangelwurzel wünschte d___ heimfahrend___Frau
   „Alles Gute".
5 Sie verdankten es ei___ kurz___ Unwetter, daß sie nicht
   hinauszugehen brauchten.

2 Declension table

A Summary of the Cases, for reference

	Nominative	Accusative	Genitive	Dative
Masculine Singular	der gute Mann ein guter Mann	den guten Mann einen guten Mann	des guten Mannes eines guten Mannes	dem guten Mann einem guten Mann
Neuter Singular	das gute Kind ein gutes Kind		des guten Kindes eines guten Kindes	dem guten Kind einem guten Kind
Feminine Singular	die gute Frau eine gute Frau		der guten Frau einer guten Frau	
Plural	die guten Leute *meine guten Leute		der guten Leute meiner guten Leute	den guten Leuten meinen guten Leuten

*mein has been used in the plural as *ein* has no plural.

Demonstrative Words (this, that etc.)

The *der, das, die* pattern and adjective endings are followed by the following demonstrative words, here shown in the nominative case.

Singular	d*er:*	dies*er* (this)	jen*er* (that)	jed*er* (each)	welch*er?* (which?)
	d*as:*	dies*es*	jen*es*	jed*es*	welch*es?*
	d*ie:*	dies*e*	jen*e*	jed*e*	welch*e?*

Plural	d*ie:*	dies*e* (these)	jen*e* (those)	all*e* (all)	welch*e?* (which?)

Note: The endings of the demonstrative words above are those which change according to the *der, das, die* case changes.

3 Possessive adjectives and 'kein'

The possessive adjectives tell you to whom the next-named object or person belongs or is related, e.g. *deine Bücher,* your books; *unser Vetter,* our cousin. The following list shows all of them, including the negative word *kein.*

mein Bruder/Hotel *meine* Schule	my brother/hotel my school	*unser*	our
dein (from 'du', see p. 29)	your	*euer* (from 'ihr', see p. 29)	your
sein	his, its (masc. and neut.)	*Ihr* (from 'Sie', see p. 29)	your
ihr	her, its (fem.)	*ihr*	their

kein	not a, no

Note 1: These words behave like *ein.* This is easily seen in the case of *mein, dein, sein* and *kein,* but less easily in the others. All

the words in all their forms are set out in the chart below, whose layout is similar to the Declension Table on p. 21.

Masculine singular — der nouns

Nominative	Accusative	Genitive	Dative
mein unser dein euer sein Ihr ihr* kein Bruder	meinen unseren deinen euren seinen Ihren ihren keinen Bruder	meines unseres deines eures seines Ihres ihres keines Bruders	meinem unserem deinem eurem seinem Ihrem ihrem keinem Bruder

Neuter singular — das nouns

Nominative	Accusative	Genitive	Dative
mein dein sein ihr* Buch	unser euer Ihr kein	meines unseres deines eures seines Ihres ihres keines Buchs	meinem unserem deinem eurem seinem Ihrem ihrem keinem Buch

Feminine singular — die nouns

Nominative	Accusative	Genitive	Dative
meine deine seine ihre* Schule	unsere eure Ihre keine	meiner deiner seiner ihrer Schule	unserer eurer Ihrer keiner

Plural — all genders

Nominative	Accusative	Genitive	Dative
meine deine seine ihre* Kinder	unsere eure Ihre keine	meiner unserer deiner eurer seiner Ihrer ihrer keiner Kinder	meinen unseren deinen euren seinen Ihren ihren keinen Kindern

*ihr - 'her' and ihr - 'their' have exactly the same forms throughout and so only one has been printed in the table.

Note 2: An adjective following one of these words in the singular will have the same ending as it would have if it followed *ein* (see declension table on p. 21), e.g. nominative singular *der* word: mein gut*er* Freund (der Freund).
   A plural adjective after one of these words will end in —*en* in all four cases (as shown in the table on p. 21, following *mein**).

23

Exercises

A

Using the words given in brackets, translate the English portion of each sentence, and copy the whole sentence.

1 Hier ist/my modest little house. (bescheiden; das Haus)
2 Es war das Auto/of our new teacher. (der Lehrer)
3 His elder sister/arbeitet in einer Fabrik. (älter)
4 Ich kann/no good reason/sehen. (der Grund)
5 Sie konnte/with her old pen/nicht schreiben. (der Füller)
6 Ich sage euch, Kinder,/your long essays/habe ich noch nicht korrigiert. (der Aufsatz, ⁻e)
7 Nun, Fräulein Schreiner, wir brauchen ein Muster/of your usual signature,/bitte. (üblich; die Unterschrift)
8 Your English friend/ist im Wohnzimmer, Udo. (englisch; der Freund)
9 Sie gaben/their hungry children/die Butterbrote. (hungrig; das Kind, ⁻er)
10 Ich ging mit/my new girlfriend/spazieren. (die Freundin)
11 Wir sprachen/with our kind neighbours. (freundlich; der Nachbar, ⁻n)
12 Gib das/(to) your naughty brother, Karin. (unartig; der Bruder)
13 Wir besuchten/her sick mother. (krank; die Mutter)
14 Er ging/into your smart living room,/Herr Priem. (schick; das Wohnzimmer)
15 In front of his modern hotel/standen viele Autos.

B

In the following two pieces of German, all the possessive adjectives and *kein* have been left out. The missing words are printed at the end, but not in the order in which they are to be replaced. Copy the two pieces in full, with the gaps filled.

a) ‚Hallo, Herr Schmidt,‘ sagte Herr Meyer. ‚Ich habe ____ Bleistift nicht. Darf ich____ Bleistift nehmen, bitte?‘
   ‚Ja,‘ antwortete Herr Schmidt. ‚Hier ist ____ Bleistift. Übrigens, wo ist____ Frau heute?‘
   ‚____ Frau ist zu Hause,‘ sagte Herr Meyer. ‚____ Tochter wohnt diese Woche bei uns, und Helga hat viel Arbeit. Die Tochter hat____ zwei Kinder mitgebracht, aber____ Mann ist nicht hier, sondern in England.‘

b) ‚Hans und Uschi, wo sind___ Schuhe?' fragt Frau Müller.
‚Hans, das ist___ Schuh, nicht wahr?' fragt Uschi. ‚Ja,'
antwortet Hans, ‚und___ Schuhe sind dort. Hier kommt
___ Klassenkamerad, Gerd. Sieh, er hat___ Hund an der Leine.'
‚___ Eltern wohnen neben uns, nicht wahr?'
‚Ja,' sagt Hans. ‚Schade, daß wir___ Hund haben.'
Hans und Uschi sagen___ Mutter ‚Auf Wiedersehen.'

---

seinen, unsere, mein, keinen, ihrer, Ihre, deine, meinen,
seine, ihr, meine, Ihren, unser, dein, ihre, eure
(Each word to be used once only.)

---

4 Personal pronouns

Form

	Nominative (subject)		Accusative (direct object)		Dative (indirect object)	
	ich	I	mich	me	mir	to me
	du	you (sing.)	dich	you (sing.)	dir	to you (sing.)
Box I	er	he, it	ihn	him, it	ihm	to him, it
	sie	she, it	sie	her, it	ihr	to her, it
	es	it	es	it	ihm	to it
	wir	we	uns	us	uns	to us
	ihr, Sie	you (pl.)	euch, Sie	you (pl.)	euch, Ihnen	to you (pl.)
Box II	sie	they	sie	them	ihnen	to them

Usage

1 Although the genitive forms exist, they are hardly ever used.
2 See also notes on *du, ihr, Sie* on p. 29.
3 If there are two objects in a sentence, the order is as follows:
   A If both are nouns, the dative (indirect) comes before the
   accusative (direct).

   Thomas schenkte seiner Freundin einen Pelzmantel.
   (Thomas gave a fur coat to his girlfriend.)
   Remember: 'NDA': (Nouns: Dative before Accusative).

25

B If both are pronouns, the accusative (direct) comes before the dative (indirect).

Thomas schenkte ihn ihr.
(Thomas gave it to her.)
Remember: 'PAD': (Pronouns: Accusative before Dative)

C If one is a noun, and the other a pronoun, the pronoun always comes before the noun.

Thomas schenkte ihn seiner Freundin.
(Thomas gave it to his girlfriend.)

Thomas schenkte ihr einen Pelzmantel.
(Thomas gave her a fur coat.)
Remember: 'MPN' (Mixture: Pronoun before Noun).

4 The third person personal pronouns are the ones most used (i.e. those in boxes I and II) and the exercises concentrate solely on those.
5 The subject (nominative) personal pronouns are also used with verbs (see subject words, p. 28).
6 When a noun is later replaced by a pronoun, the pronoun must be chosen from either box I or box II above, using I for a singular noun, II for a plural one. The chosen pronoun must have the same gender as its noun if it is taken from box I. The case of the pronoun will depend on how it is used in its own sentence.

Exercises

A

To test the use of the third person pronouns and the order of objects.
E.g. Onkel Otto gab seinem jungen Neffen das Buch.
This sentence is to be rewritten three times, each time changing an underlined phrase to a pronoun. Work in sequence.

   a) Er gab seinem jungen Neffen das Buch.
   b) Onkel Otto gab ihm das Buch.
   c) Onkel Otto gab es seinem jungen Neffen.

Now do the same for the following three sentences. (Note that the pronouns in these sentences will have to be in the same case as the nouns which they replace. Note also that when a noun becomes a pronoun, it loses any article or adjective that stood in front of it.)

1 Tante Liesl zeigte den Kindern die schöne Blume.
2 Der reiche Mann schenkte seiner Heimatstadt sein großes Grundstück.
3 Das junge Mädchen schickte ihrem älteren Bruder die zwei Ansichtskarten.

Now do a fourth sentence for each of the above, in which the last two phrases are changed into pronouns. Remember 'PAD': E.g. Onkel Otto gab es ihm.

Lastly, a fifth sentence to show all three changed into pronouns.

B

In the following sentences, gaps have been left where pronouns should be. Write the numbers 1-8, and against each number write the correct pronoun, taken from box I or II in the chart on p. 25.

1 Diese Schuhe sind zu klein. ____ tun meinen Füßen weh.
2 Onkel Hermann ist gekommen. Mit ____ gehen wir ins Kino.
3 ‚Hast du einen Bleistift?‘ ‚Nein, ich habe ____ leider verloren.‘
4 Da kommt Mutti. Gib ____ das Buch, das du gekauft hast.
5 Ich habe Freunde in Berlin, aber seit drei Wochen habe ich von ____ nichts gehört.
6 ‚Ist das dein Pferd?‘ ‚Ja, ____ war ein Geschenk von meinem Vater.‘
7 ‚Das ist Fräulein Lehmke. Gestern sah ich ____ mit meinem Vetter im Park.‘
8 ‚Wo sind meine beiden Brüder?‘ ‚Ich sah ____ gerade aus der Schule kommen.‘

5 Subject words

(See also Introduction p. 3 'The Sentence'). All these words may be used with a verb in German.

Singular

	ich	I
	du	you (to friend or family)
	[er]	he

	er	it (referring to der words)
	sie	she
All take	*sie*	it (referring to die words)
same verb	*es*	it (referring to das words)
part as	*der/ein* + noun	the/a/an
[er]	*das/ein* + noun	the/a/an
	die/eine + noun	the/a/an
	man	one, you, people in general
	(*Anton*)	(single name of someone)
	wer?	who?

Plural

	wir	we
	ihr	you (to several friends, members of family)
	Sie	you (to one or more than one person)
	[sie]	they

All take	*die* + plural noun	the . . .s
same verb	(*Hans und Anton*)	(more than one named person)
part as	*mehrere, alle,*	several, all, which? etc.
[sie]	*welche?* etc. +	+ plural nouns without an
	plural nouns	article
	without an article	

28

Only seven parts are usually shown when a verb is written out:

ich	(I)	*wir*	(we)
du	(you)	*ihr*	(you)
		Sie	(you)
er	(he/ it)	sie	(they)

er (singular) and sie (plural) are always shown boxed to remind you that several other subject words take the same verb part (as shown opposite).

6 Du, ihr, Sie

These are all personal pronouns meaning 'you'. For their accusative and dative forms, see the full chart of personal pronouns (p. 25).

Usage

a) *du* is used to address an intimate friend, a relative, a child or a pet. The ending on the verb is —*st:*
‚Helene, *hast du* mein Buch?'

b) *ihr* is the plural form of *du*, and is used where more than one friend, relative, child or pet is being addressed. The ending on the verb is —*t:* ‚Kinder! Morgen *macht ihr* einen Ausflug an die See.'

c) *Sie* (always written with a capital letter) is used to address one or more persons who are strangers or superiors, or not on close terms with the speaker. The verb ending is —*en* (except for the present tense of *sein*, to be; see p. 32).
‚Frau Holm, *Sie kennen* meinen Sohn, nicht wahr?'
‚Meine Herrschaften, *nehmen Sie* bitte Platz.'

Exercises

A

Copy the numbers 1-10. Study the following sentences and decide which of the nine pronouns in the boxes below fits best in each case. Write it against the number.

Nominative	Accusative	Dative
du	dich	dir
ihr	euch	euch
Sie	Sie	Ihnen

1 'You (1) haven't done your homework,' said the teacher to his class.
2 'Sorry, sir, you (2) didn't set any,' said the form representative.
3 'Are you (3) sure of that, Peter?' asked the teacher. Then he turned to the class. 'Are you (4) all quite sure?'
4 'It's the third time you (5) forgot to set it,' said another boy.
5 'I surely don't have to remind you (6), do I?' said the teacher to the representative.
6 'I wasn't here that day. I told [+ dative] you (7) yesterday, sir. I was at the dentist's,' said the form rep. and, looking around the class, said, 'Can't I trust (+ dative) you (8) to remind him?'
7 'He'll give us extra work now,' growled one of the class. 'I'll get you (9) after school, Peter, and I'll give [+ dative] you (10) something to remember!'

B

Copy the following sentences, filling in the appropriate form of *du, ihr* or *Sie.*
1 Ich habe ___ nicht gesehen, seitdem ___ deinen Unfall gehabt hast. Komm, ich will ___ etwas geben.
2 Kommen ___ bitte herein, mein lieber Kollege, und setzen ___ sich! Wie geht es ___?
3 ‚Maria, was hast ___ getan?‘ fragte die Lehrerin. Dann sagte sie zu der Klasse: ‚Ich gebe ___ allen zwei Minuten, dann

müßt ihr mir die Wahrheit [truth] sagen. Kinder, habt ____
gesehen, was Maria getan hat?'

4 ‚Heinrich, ____ bist unartig,' sagte der Vater, und wandte
sich zu dem Herrn: ‚Entschuldigen ____ ihn, bitte.'

5 , ____ und ich, wir können ins Kino gehen,' sagte Franz zu
seiner Freundin.

Part III

7 Sein, haben & werden

a) *Sein*, 'to be' (followed by nominative case)

Present		*Imperfect* (simple past)		*Perfect* (compound past)	
ich bin	I am	ich war	I was	ich bin gewesen	I was, have been
du bist	you are	du warst	you were	du bist gewesen	you were, have been
er ist	he/it is	er war	he/it was	er ist gewesen	he was, has been
wir sind	we are	wir waren	we were	wir sind gewesen	we were, have been
ihr seid	you are	ihr wart	you were	ihr seid gewesen	you were, have been
Sie sind	you are	Sie waren	you were	Sie sind gewesen	you were, have been
sie sind	they are	sie waren	they were	sie sind gewesen	they were, have been

b) *Haben*, 'to have' (followed by accusative case)

Present		*Imperfect*		*Perfect*	
ich habe	I have	ich hatte	I had	ich habe gehabt	I had, have had
du hast	you have	du hattest	you had	du hast gehabt	you had, have had
er hat	he/it has	er hatte	he had	er hat gehabt	he had, has had
wir haben	we have	wir hatten	we had	wir haben gehabt	we had, have had
ihr habt	you have	ihr hattet	you had	ihr habt gehabt	you had, have had
Sie haben	you have	Sie hatten	you had	Sie haben gehabt	you had, have had
sie haben	they have	sie hatten	they had	sie haben gehabt	they had, have had

c) *Werden*, 'to become' (followed by nominative case)

Present		Imperfect	
ich werde	I become	ich wurde	I became
du wirst	you become	du wurdest	you became
er wird	he/it becomes	er wurde	he became
wir werden	we become	wir wurden	we became
ihr werdet	you become	ihr wurdet	you became
Sie werden	you become	Sie wurden	you became
sie werden	they become	sie wurden	they became

Perfect	
ich bin geworden	I became, have become
du bist geworden	you became, have become
er ist geworden	he became, has become
wir sind geworden	we became, have become
ihr seid geworden	you became, have become
Sie sind geworden	you became, have become
sie sind geworden	they became, have become

Note: 1 These three verbs are the 'foundation' verbs of the German language. Apart from being used on their own (meanings given above), they are used with other verbs to form tenses.

Haben and *sein* are used to form the perfect and pluperfect tenses (see p. 48), e.g. Ich *habe/hatte* geraucht. Sie *ist/war* gelaufen.

Werden forms the future and conditional tenses (see p. 52), e.g. Ich *werde* kommen. Sie *würde* gern singen. It is also used to form the passive, dealt with on p. 65.

Note: 2 a) *Haben* is followed by a direct object, in the accusative case: Er hat *einen Bleistift.*

b) *Sein* and *werden* are followed, not by an object, but by a complement, in the nominative case:

Mein Vater ist *ein guter Sänger.*
Vetter Franz wurde *ein reicher Mann.*

33

Why are *Sänger* and *Mann* in the nominative, which is usually reserved for the subject of the sentence (here *Mein Vater* and *Vetter Franz*)? Because the *complement* is the *same person* as the subject: *Mein Vater = ein guter Sänger, Vetter Franz = ein reicher Mann,* and so goes into the same case as the subject.

Exercises

A

Write down the numbers 1-10, and against each number write the correct part of *haben, sein* or *werden*, according to the English meaning given.

1. ‚Ich (am) müde,‘ sagte er.
2. Wir (became) sehr ungeduldig.
3. Wo (were) ihr gestern Abend?
4. Sie [you] (had) Glück.
5. Du (have become) berühmt.
6. Sie [they] (have been) den ganzen Sommer über in Bonn.
7. (Have) du eine bessere Idee?
8. Er (is) sehr stolz auf seinen Sohn.
9. Es (becomes) immer schwieriger.
10. Ich (was) traurig.

B

Copy the sentences that follow, putting in the appropriate part of *haben, sein* or *werden*, in the appropriate tense and form. IMP indicates that the imperfect (simple past) tense should be used.

‚___ du heute beim Einkaufen Glück gehabt?‘
‚Ja, ich IMP sehr früh in der Stadt. Ich — im Kaufhaus gewesen, und — [use *haben*] ein schönes Kleid gekauft. Plötzlich — der Himmel dunkel geworden. Nicht viele Autos IMP auf der Straße, aber ein Taxi — [use *sein*] auf mich zugefahren. ‚Sie — Glück!‘ sagte der Fahrer.‘

Mit achtzehn Jahren, IMP Maria schon eine fleißige Studentin.
Mit zwanzig Jahren IMP Maria einen netten Freund namens Kurt.
Mit zweiundzwanzig Jahren IMP Maria Kurts Frau.

34

8 Present tense

Infinitive Form

The infinitive of a verb is the form you find in a dictionary or a
verb list or in a vocabulary. It is that part which means 'to' do
something.

to run	laufen	
to change	wechseln	} all ending in *—en* or *—n*
to hike	wandern	

The *—en* or *—n* is always removed before any other tense
endings are added. The infinitive without the ending is called the
stem of the verb. The stems of the examples used above are:

lauf-   *wechsel-*   *wander-*

Present Tense: Formation

Regular

All weak verbs and some strong ones, e.g. *gehen* and *kommen*
are regular in the present tense. See strong verb list (present
tense) pp 70-76.

1 Take the infinitive, e.g. *kommen*
2 Remove *—en* to get the stem: *komm—*
3 Add the ending which goes with *ich, du, er* etc.

kommen		finden	
ich komme	I come, am coming	ich finde	I find
du kommst	you come	du findest[2]	you find
er kommt	he/it comes	er findet[2]	he finds
wir kommen	we come	wir finden	we find
ihr kommt	you come	ihr findet[2]	you find
Sie kommen	you come	Sie finden	you find
sie kommen	they come	sie finden	they find

35

Note:
1 The endings in *italics* are the same for all regular and irregular verbs.
2 Notice that an extra *e* is added if the stem of a verb ends in —*d*, —*n* or —*t* in the *du*, *er* and *ihr* forms, before the normal ending is added (see the example of *finden*). This applies to *öffnen* (to open), *regnen* (to rain), etc. as well.

Irregular

Some strong verbs have an irregular present tense, and these fall into three main groups because the stem changes in one of three ways, and this change only affects the *du* and *er* forms of the present tense. However, all the endings are the same as for regular verbs.

1 *a (au)* changes to *ä (äu)* (in the *du* and *er* forms only)

backen (to bake)	laufen (to run)
ich backe	ich laufe
du bäckst	du läufst
er bäckt	er läuft

All of the following verbs change in the same way:

blasen	to blow	laden	to load
braten	to roast	lassen	to leave
einladen	to invite	raten	to guess
fahren	to travel	schlafen	to sleep
fallen	to fall	schlagen	to hit
fangen	to catch	tragen	to carry; to wear
graben	to dig	wachsen	to grow
halten	to stop; to hold	waschen	to wash

Stoßen (to push) changes in a similar way: the *o* becomes *ö* in the *du* and *er* forms.

2 *e* changes to *i* (in the *du* and *er* forms only)

brechen (to break)	sterben (to die)
ich breche	ich sterbe
du br*i*chst	du st*i*rbst
er br*i*cht	er st*i*rbt

36

All of the following verbs change in the same way:

erschrecken	to scare	schelten	to scold
essen	to eat	schmelzen	to melt
fressen	to eat, devour	stechen	to prick, sting
geben	to give	treffen	to meet
gelten	to be worth	verderben	to spoil
helfen	to help	vergessen	to forget
messen	to measure	werfen	to throw

Note also: nehmen (to take), er nimmt

3 e changes to ie (in the du and er forms only)

befehlen (to order, command)   lesen (to read)
ich befehle   ich lese
du befiehlst   du liest
er befiehlt   er liest

All of the following verbs change in the same way:

empfehlen	to recommend	sehen	to see
geschehen	to happen	stehlen	to steal

Exercises

A *(regular)*

Complete the following sentences by putting the correct ending on the verb:

1 Wie komm__ ich am besten zum Bahnhof, bitte?
2 Wir kauf__ Wein in der Kaufhalle.
3 Es steh__ in der Bahnhofstraße.
4 Geh__ ihr mit ins Kino?
5 Der Briefträger bring__ uns eine Karte aus England.
6 Mein Vater arbeit__ in einer Fabrik.
7 Die Dame find__ keinen Platz im Zug.
8 Dann bind__ du das Boot fest.
9 ‚Keine Sorge,‘ antwort__ der Mann lächelnd.
10 Er öffn__ die Tür.

B *(irregular)*

Complete the following sentences by putting the verb in the correct form: refer to the irregular sections of the present tense.

1 Wann (fahren) du nach England?
2 Du (sehen) es doch nicht.
3 Er (lesen) die Zeitung.
4 Das Auto (halten) an der Ampel.
5 Der Dieb (stehlen) immer von reichen Leuten.
6 Meine Frau (nehmen) 'Spüli' zum Abwaschen.
7 Es (fangen) an zu regnen.
8 Paul (helfen) immer seinem Vater.
9 Ihr (laufen) zu schnell!
10 Der Mann (treffen) ins Ziel.

9 Imperfect tense

This *one-word* past tense in German is commonly used in stories. Notice that this one-word past is used for the four English forms of the past tense shown below:

> I came
> I used to come   To say any of these in German simply
> I did come   use *ich kam*
> I was coming

In the imperfect tense, verbs are one of two main types:
1 Strong: where they change their vowel and do not take regular endings, e.g. *kommen* (to come); *er kam* (he came).
2 Weak: where there is no vowel change and regular endings are used for every weak past tense.

A few verbs are mixed (see strong verb list, p. 71, section 3).

Strong Verbs

You must check all verbs against the list on pp 70-76 to see if they are strong. The imperfect tense is given in the er form: e.g. *brechen, brach,* and the endings are as follows:

ich brach	wir brach*en*
du brach*st*	ihr brach*t*
er brach	Sie brach*en*
	sie brach*en*

Note: *ich* and *er* forms have no endings; *du* has *—st; ihr* has *—t;*
wir, Sie and *sie* (plural) have *—en.*

Weak Verbs

Take the infinitive, e.g. *kaufen, antworten, basteln,* remove the
ending *—en* (or *—n*), and add the past tense endings (in italic)
below.

ich	kauf*te*	wir	kauf*ten*
du	kauf*test*	ihr	kauf*tet*
er	kauf*te*	Sie	kauf*ten*
		sie	kauf*ten*

Note: with *—d, —n* and *—t* stems, e.g. arbei*ten,* an extra *—e* must
be inserted before the past endings, e.g. ich arbei*te*te, du
arbei*te*test etc.

Examples using strong and weak verbs

1 Der Zeitungsverkäufer *stand* an der Ecke.
(The newspaper seller was standing on the corner.)

2 Er *arbeitete* in einer Fabrik.
(He used to work in a factory.)

3 Frau Braun *ging* in den Supermarkt.
(Frau Braun went into the supermarket.)

4 Der Hund *bellte* laut.
(The dog barked loudly.)

Exercises

A *(Weak verbs)*
Put the verb given in brackets in its correct past tense form.

1 Wir (machen) unsere Hausaufgaben.
2 Der Direktor (stellen) seinen Stuhl in die Ecke.
3 Johann (legen) sein Buch auf den Tisch.
4 Mutter (probieren) das Bananeneis.
5 Hans und Julia (holen) die Gläser aus dem Schrank.

(Strong verbs) (Refer to table pp 70-76).

1   Ich (kommen) zu spät in die Schule.
2   Vater (liegen) in seinem Liegestuhl.
3   Die zwei Kinder (sein) müde.
4   Wir (bringen) zwei Freunde mit.
5   Die Frau (lesen) die neuesten Nachrichten in der Zeitung.

(Both) (Check each verb in the strong verb list first)

1   Wir (fallen) vom Baum herunter.
2   Sie [she] (geben) ihm ihr Geld.
3   Ich (fegen) das Schlafzimmer aus.
4   Das Auto (stoppen) am Fußgängerübergang.
5. Die Biene (stechen) das Kind in den Arm.
6. Er (bringen) seine Butterbrote mit.
7   Michael und Johann (gehen) in den Wald.
8   Sie [they] (schauen) sich das Fußballspiel an.
9   Die Kinder (laufen) schnell zur Schule.
10 Der Polizist (klopfen) an die Tür.

B

Translate the verb into German (check each one to see if it is strong.)

1   Hans und Johann (went) auf das Land.
2   Wir (went) mit dem Zug nach London.
3   Du (brought) ihn mit, nicht wahr?
4   Er (ate) Erbsensuppe, Schinken und Kartoffeln.
5   Die Männer (put) die Tassen auf den Tisch.

10 Modal verbs

There are six modal verbs in German:

dürfen	to be able (to do something), i.e. permitted
können	to be able (to do something), i.e. capable
müssen	to have (to do something)

sollen	to be expected (to do something), to be supposed to				
wollen	to want (to do something)				
mögen	to like (doing something)				

Note the difference between *dürfen* and *können*:

‚Ich *kann* Fußball spielen, aber ich *darf* es nicht.'
('I *can* play football, but I'm not *allowed* to'.)

‚*Darf* dein Bruder spielen?' ‚Ja, aber er *kann* es nicht.'
('Can your brother play?' [permission] 'Yes, but he doesn't know how to.' [ability])

Modal verbs show the mood of the sentence: wanting to, liking, having to, etc., and are usually supported by another verb. This second verb remains in its infinitive form and goes to the end of the sentence or clause.

Ich *will* Fußball *spielen*. (I want to play football.)
Ich *muß* Fußball *spielen*. (I have to play football.)

Note how the mood or tone of the sentence is changed by the modal verb, and that it sends the infinitive of the second verb, *spielen*, to the end of the sentence.

Present Tense

	dürfen	*können*	*müssen*	*sollen*	*wollen*	*mögen*
	can (allowed to)	can (able to)	must, have to	should be, expected to	want	like
ich	darf	kann	muß	soll	will	mag
du	darfst	kannst	mußt	sollst	willst	magst
er	darf	kann	muß	soll	will	mag
wir	dürfen	können	müssen	sollen	wollen	mögen
ihr	dürft	könnt	müßt	sollt	wollt	mögt
Sie	dürfen	können	müssen	sollen	wollen	mögen
sie	dürfen	können	müssen	sollen	wollen	mögen

Note: 1. The *ich* form in all modal verbs in the same as the *er* form.

2. *Mögen* is usually met with in the following special forms meaning "would like to":

ich möchte   wir möchten
du möchtest   ihr möchtet
er möchte   Sie möchten
                sie möchten

3. A verb of motion may be omitted with a modal verb:
Wir möchten nach Spanien.

Examples

Er kann schwimmen. (He can swim.)
Du darfst hier nicht *rauchen.* (You can't smoke here.)
Sie müssen nicht bei ihr *bleiben.* (You don't have to stay with her.)
Wir sollen an unsere Eltern *schreiben.* (We should write to our parents.)
Ich will sie *sehen.* (I want to see them.)
Er möchte nach Deutschland. (He would like to go to Germany.)

Exercises

A

Put the correct form of the verb in the following sentences:

1 ‚Nein, Kinder, ihr (dürfen) nicht draußen spielen.'
2 Hans (können) gut Fußball spielen.
3 Petra und Monika (sollen) sofort zum Direktor kommen.
4 Vater (müssen) zur Arbeit gehen.
5 Ich (wollen) ein Eis essen.

B

Choose the correct modal verb part for each sentence.

1 Mein Bruder ist sportlich und (muß/will/kann) immer Fußball spielen.
2 Kinder (wollen/dürfen/sollen) immer Bonbons essen.
3 Man (soll/will/darf) eine Strafe gleich bezahlen.
4 Die Dame kommt zu spät ins Theater und sie (möchte/kann/muß) draußen warten.
5 In einem Nichtraucher (kann/darf/muß) man nicht rauchen.

Imperfect Tense

können, dürfen, sollen, wollen and *müssen* all have a weak (regular) imperfect tense, although all umlauts disappear. With *mögen* the —*g*—, changes to —*ch*—, and then it takes weak imperfect tense endings and also loses its umlaut.

dürfen	er *durfte*	(could)
können	er *konnte*	(could)
müssen	er *mußte*	(had to)
sollen	er *sollte*	(was to)
wollen	er *wollte*	(wanted to)
mögen	er *mochte*	(liked — doing something)

Examples

1 *Wir wollten* den Film *sehen.* (We wanted to see the film.)
2 *Er mußte* nach Hause *gehen.*   (He had to go home.)

Exercises

A

Put the correct ending on the modal verb in each of the following:

1 Ich moch___ nicht mit ihm spielen.
2 Wir muß___ zur Arbeit gehen.
3 Sie [she] woll___ schlafen.
4 Sie [they] soll___ arbeiten.
5 ‚Konn ___ du nicht den Baum sehen?‘

B

Put the modal verb into the past tense.

1 Das Schauspiel war so lustig. Wir (müssen) lachen.
2 Die Dame (können) ihren Koffer nicht herunterholen.
3 Die Kinder waren so müde, aber sie (wollen) nicht ins Bett gehen.
4 Ich (dürfen) die Zigaretten nicht nach England bringen.
5 ‚Was (sollen) du denn machen? Du (können) doch nichts dafür!‘
6 Er (dürfen) nicht vor dem Rathaus parken.
7 Mein Vater (wollen) meine Hausaufgaben|sehen.

43

8 Sie (können) machen, was Sie (wollen).
9 Ich (müssen) arbeiten.
10 Sie [she] (sollen) um neun Uhr ankommen.

B

Put the following into German.

1 He had to go to school.
2 We were not allowed to play in the street.
3 The policeman could not find the car.
4 They are to arrive at four o'clock.
5 Maria and Susanne wanted to go by train.

11 Reflexive verbs

A reflexive verb is one which has a reflexive pronoun, shown in dictionaries and vocabularies as *sich*.

E.g.　*sich waschen*　—　to get washed, to wash oneself

There are two patterns of reflexive pronouns, as shown in the table below.

Accusative	*Dative*
ich wasche *mich*	ich wasche *mir* die Hände
du wäschst *dich*	du wäschst *dir* die Hände
er wäscht *sich*	er wäscht *sich* die Hände
wir waschen *uns*	wir waschen *uns* die Hände
ihr wascht *euch*	ihr wascht *euch* die Hände
Sie waschen *sich*	Sie waschen *sich* die Hände
sie waschen *sich*	sie waschen *sich* die Hände

Accusative reflexive pronoun is used:

With verbs showing what the subject does itself. With these verbs it is impossible to have another word in the accusative as a direct

44

object. The reflexive pronoun in effect stands as a direct object.

E.g. Ich ruhe *mich* aus — I have a rest (i.e. rest myself)

Er wäscht *sich* — He gets washed (i.e. washes himself)

Dative reflexive pronoun is used:

1 When two or more people involve each other in the verb.

E.g. Sie trosteten *sich* gegenseitig.
(They comforted each other.)

Wir sahen *uns* einen Augenblick an.
(We looked at each other for a moment.)

2 When an action is done for the self or to part of the self.

E.g. Ich wusch *mir* die Hände
(I washed my hands.)

Er kämmte *sich* das Haar
(He combed his hair.)

Hast du *dir* ein neues Auto gekauft?
(Have you bought yourself a new car?)

Also in this section is the expression:

sich etwas machen *lassen* — to have something done

E.g. *Er läßt sich* einen neuen Anzug *machen.*
(He is having a new suit made.)

Ich ließ mir das Auto *waschen.*
(I had my car washed.)

Note: The use of dative reflexive pronoun is only apparent in the *ich* (*mir*) and *du* (*dir*) forms. Otherwise the form is exactly the same as in the accusative.

Position of the Reflexive Pronoun

The rule is that the reflexive pronoun goes as near to the subject as possible, without breaking any other rule of word order (see note below.)

E.g. Er legte *sich* auf sein Bett, weil er *sich* nicht wohl fühlte.
(He lay down on his bed, because he did not feel well.)

Dann legte er *sich* auf sein Bett.
(Then he lay down on his bed.)

When the reflexive verb is used in an infinitive construction, the reflexive pronoun must still change in form to reflect the subject.

E.g. Du mußt *dich bemühen*, früh aufzustehen.
(You must make an effort to get up early.)

Ich versuchte, *mich* ein bißchen *auszuruhen*.
(I tried to rest a bit.)

Note: When a noun is used instead of a pronoun as the subject in a secondary clause, the reflexive pronoun often comes between the conjunction and the subject (but this is purely style and *not a rule*).

E.g. Als *sich* der Junge auf das Bett legte, fühlte er sich unwohl.
(When the boy lay down on the bed, he did not feel well.)

Common Reflexive Verbs

Abbreviations: str. = strong verb acc. = accusative
(see list dat. = dative
p. 70) gen. = genitive
sep. = separable
insep. = inseparable

sich ängstigen	to become anxious
sich ängstigen (um + acc.)	to worry (about)
sich anstrengen (sep.)	to make an effort
sich anziehen (sep.)	to get dressed
sich ärgern (über + acc.)	to get annoyed (about)
sich aufregen (über + acc.) (sep.)	to get excited (about)
sich ausruhen (sep.)	to have a rest
sich ausziehen (sep.)	to get undressed
sich bedanken (bei + dat.) (insep.)	to say thank you (to)
sich beeilen (insep.)	to hurry
sich befinden (str. insep.)	to be (situated)
sich bemühen (um + acc.) (insep.)	to care (for); to try to obtain
sich bemühen (etwas zu machen) (insep.)	to take the trouble (to do something)
sich beschäftigen (mit + dat.) (insep.)	to devote oneself to; to spend time doing

46

sich entscheiden (für + acc.) (str. insep.)	to decide (on something)
sich entschließen (zu + dat.) (str. insep.)	to decide (on something)
sich entschließen (etwas zu machen). (str. insep.)	to decide (to do something)
sich entschuldigen (bei + dat.) (insep.)	to apologise (to a person)
sich entschuldigen (wegen + dat) (insep.)	to apologise (for something)
sich entwickeln (insep.)	to develop
sich erholen (insep.)	to recover (from an illness)
sich erinnern (an + acc.) (insep.)	to remember (something)
sich freuen (über + acc.)	to be pleased (about something)
sich freuen (auf + acc.)	to look forward (to something)
sich hinlegen (sep.)	to lie down
sich interessieren (für + acc.)	to be interested (in)
sich (dat.) das Haar kämmen	to comb one's hair
sich kleiden	to dress (well, badly etc.)
sich melden (zu + dat.)	to report (to reception, office etc.), to present oneself (at)
sich nähern (+ dat.)	to move near (to something)
sich öffnen	to open (i.e. 'the door opens') (compare *öffnen* — to open something)
sich rasieren	to have a shave
sich setzen	to sit down
sich umkleiden (sep.)	to get changed
sich umsehen (str. sep.)	to look around one
sich umziehen (str. sep.)	to get changed
sich unterhalten (str. insep.)	to converse with, entertain one another
sich verfahren (str. insep.)	to lose one's way (in car etc.)
sich verlassen (auf + acc) (str. insep.)	to rely (on)
sich verstehen (str. insep.)	to get on with one another
sich vorstellen (sep.)	to introduce oneself
sich (dat.) (etwas) vorstellen (sep.)	to imagine (something)
sich wohl fühlen	to feel well; to feel at home
sich wundern (über + acc.)	to be surprised (at)

12 Perfect tense

Formation

To form the perfect tense, use the present tense of *haben* (with some verbs use the present of *sein*) with the past participle of the verb concerned.

haben	
ich habe	wir haben
du hast	ihr habt
er hat	Sie haben
	sie haben

sein	
ich bin	wir sind
du bist	ihr seid
er ist	Sie sind
	sie sind

Most verbs which take *sein* in the perfect tense are strong verbs. For those verbs which take *sein*, the perfect tense er form is shown in the last column of the strong verb list (pp 70-76) as follows: e.g. laufen, *ist* gelaufen.

Past Participle

Weak (regular)	spielen	to play	*ge*-spiel-*t*
	wohnen	to live	*ge*-wohn-*t*
	fragen	to ask	*ge*-frag-*t*
	kaufen	to buy	*ge*-kauf-*t*

Note: 1 -*en* is removed from the infinitive.
2 *ge*- is added to the front and -*t* added to the end of the stem.

Strong	trinken	to drink	*ge*-trunk-*en*
	finden	to find	*ge*-fund-*en*
	reißen	to tear	*ge*-riss-*en*

48

Note: The only general rule which usually applies to strong verbs is that the past participle begins with the normal *ge-* and ends in *-en*, but check in the strong verb list (last column) where the past participle for each strong verb is given. Note also the special sections 1, 2 and 3 of the strong verb list (pp. 70-71) and also the note on modal verbs at the end of this section (p. 50).

Points to Watch

1 Verbs with *separable* prefixes (*an-*, *auf-*, *ab-*, *vor-*, etc.) sandwich the '*-ge-*' between the prefix and the verb.

*vor*stellen	to introduce, present	vor-*ge*-stell-*t*	} weak
*an*hören	to listen to	an-*ge*-hör-*t*	
*vor*fahren	to drive up	vor-*ge*-fahren	} strong
*auf*heben	to raise, lift up	auf-*ge*-hoben	

2 Verbs with *inseparable* prefixes (*be-*, *emp-*, *ent-*, *ge-*, *hinter-*, *er-*, *miß-* , *ver-*, *zer-*) do not take the extra prefix '*ge-*' for the past participle.

*be*suchen	to visit	*be*sucht	} weak (end-
*ent*decken	to discover	*ent*deckt	ing *-t*)
*be*fehlen	to command	*be*fohlen	} strong (end-
*ver*lieren	to lose	*ver*loren	ing *-en*)

(For a list of inseparable verbs, see pp 58-60)

3 Verbs of *French origin* ending in '*-ieren*', e.g. stud*ieren*, to study; kompon*ieren*, to compose (music etc.), do not add the prefix '*ge-*'. E.g. studier*t*; komponier*t*.

4 Weak verbs which have a stem ending in '*-d*' or '*-t*' add '*-e-*' before the final '*-t*' in past participles.

E.g. kosten	to cost	*ge*-kost-*e-t*
arbeiten	to work	*ge*-arbeit-*e-t*
landen	to land	*ge*-land-*e-t*
enden	to end	*ge*-end-*e-t*

Usage

The compound past or perfect tense is used in conversation, written dialogue and letter writing. It is used to express a *completed action* in the *past*.

Ich habe ein neues Auto *gekauft.*
(I've bought a new car.)

Mein Bruder ist ins Wasser *gefallen.*
(My brother fell into the water.)

Position of the past participle

The past participle always goes to the end of the clause or sentence (see examples on p. 49.)

Modal Verbs in the Perfect Tense (not commonly used)

1 Modal verbs remain in the infinitive to form the perfect tense, when they have another verb dependent on them (as is usually the case). Look at the following examples:
Ich *habe* es nicht *machen können*.
(I was not able to do it.)

Er *hat* seinen Bruder *mitnehmen müssen*.
(He had to take his brother with him.)

Wir *haben* den Film nicht *sehen wollen*.
(We didn't want to see the film.)

2 When a dependent or secondary verb is not used, the past participle of the modal verbs most likely to be used in this way is formed as shown below:

wollen: wir *haben* es nicht *gewollt*. (We didn't want that.)
können: sie *hat* es nicht *gekonnt*. (She couldn't.)

Note: The perfect tense of modal verbs is usually avoided. You are advised to use the simple past (imperfect) throughout. (See the section on modal verbs, p. 43).

Past Participle used as an Adjective

Der Krug war *zerbrochen*.   (The jug was broken.)
Mein Bein ist *verletzt*.   (My leg is injured.)

Note: Do not confuse this with the *perfect tense* using *sein* as a *helping verb*, and do not confuse it with the *passive* (see p. 66).

der *zerbrochene* Krug   (the broken jug)
ein *verletztes* Bein   (an injured leg)
eine frisch *gestrichene* Tür   (a freshly painted door)

Pluperfect tense

Formation

Exactly the same rules apply to the pluperfect tense as to the perfect tense except that the helping verb (auxiliaries *haben* and *sein*) are used in the imperfect rather than the present tense.

Compare these examples:

Perfect tense	*Pluperfect tense*
ich *habe* gespielt	ich *hatte* gespielt
er *ist* gekommen	er *war* gekommen

The rules for the perfect tense (p. 48) should be used, but remember to use the imperfect tense of the helping verb. (See section Sein, Haben, Werden on p. 32).

Usage

Where English would use had done something, the pluperfect tense would be used in German.

Ich betrat sein Zimmer, aber er *war* vor zehn Minuten *weggegangen.*
(I went into his room, but he had left ten minutes earlier.)

Exercises

Give the appropriate form of the perfect and pluperfect tense for the following verbs.

1   ich (laufen)
2   er (fallen)
3   wir (haben)
4   Sie (entscheiden)
5   sie [they] (verstehen)

6 es (sein)
7 die Männer (verlieren)
8 ihr (vergessen)
9 ich (gebrauchen)
10 das Mädchen (gewinnen)

13 Future tense

Formation

ich werde du wirst er wird wir werden ihr werdet Sie werden sie werden	+ infinitive of 'meaning' verb e.g. *kommen, anfangen, arbeiten,* *spielen* etc.

The present tense of *'werden'* is the main verb, which is placed second in the sentence (in fact it obeys all the rules for the verb), and the verb whose *future tense* is being formed remains in the *infinitive (-en)* form and is placed at the *end of the clause or sentence*.

Mein Freund *wird* nächstes Jahr nach Deutschland *fahren.*
(My friend will go to Germany next year.)

Usage

The future tense is simply used to say what will happen or to show what someone intends to do in the future.

,Helmut, steig von der Mauer herunter! Du *wirst* sicher *fallen,'* schrie seine Mutter.
('Helmut, get off that wall. You will fall off,' his mother shouted.)

Note: Where an infinitive is already being used, with a modal verb for example, the future tense infinitive goes to the end. Compare these two sentences:

Ich *kann* das machen. (I can do that.) (present tense)
Ich *werde* das machen *können.* (I shall be able to do that.)
     (future tense)

The future of *können* has been formed. Here are two more sentences to demonstrate the idea.

Peter *muß* sehr schwer in der Schule arbeiten. (Peter has to work very hard at school.)

Peter *wird* sehr schwer in der Schule arbeiten *müssen*. (Peter will have to work very hard at school.)

Conditional tense

Formation

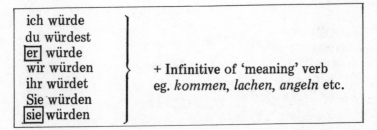

ich würde
du würdest
er würde
wir würden
ihr würdet
Sie würden
sie würden

+ Infinitive of 'meaning' verb
eg. *kommen, lachen, angeln* etc.

Note that this special tense of *werden* is now used in the same way as in the future tense, and the 'meaning' verb (i.e. the verb whose conditional tense you are forming) remains in the infinitive form as it does in the future tense, and is again placed at the end of the clause or sentence.

Ich *würde* in einem Büro *arbeiten*.
(I would work in an office.)

Usage

The conditional tense, as its name suggests, is usually linked with a conditional clause, introduced by *wenn* meaning 'if'.

Wenn er arbeitete, dann *würde* er etwas Geld *verdienen*.
(If he worked, he would earn some money.)

(For further uses of *wenn* + conditional clauses, see section on subjunctive forms, p. 64).

53

Exercises

Future tense only

A

Put the correct form of *werden* in these future tense sentences.

1 Nächstes Jahr ____wir nach Bingen umziehen.
2 Mein Vater ____ spät nach Hause kommen.
3 Ich ____ ganz böse sein.
4 Die CDU ____ gewinnen.
5 Wann ____ du zurückkommen?

B

Put the verb (in brackets) in the following sentences into the future.

1 Er (will) nicht kommen.
2 Ich (esse) nicht viel.
3 Morgen (geht) die ganze Familie ans Meer.
4 Ihr (seid) nicht enttäuscht.
5 (Können) Sie die Tür aufschließen?

14 Separable and inseparable prefixes

A prefix is a small element, often a preposition, which is fixed on to the front of a 'base verb'. The prefix is in *italics* in the following examples.

*emp*fehlen   *beein*drucken   *mit*bringen

The prefix may be one of two types, each dealt with separately in this section.
The types of prefix are:

1 *Separable:*   meaning that they do not always remain prefixed to the base verb but separate from it, moving to the end of the clause or sentence.

2 *Inseparable:* meaning that they *cannot separate* from the base verb but remain prefixed at all times.

Note that there are some prefixes which are used both as separable and as inseparable, and fuller notes on these are given at the end of the section on inseparable prefixes (p. 60).

Separable Prefixes

ab-	abbrechen	to break off
an-	annehmen	to accept; to assume
auf-	aufhören	to cease, stop
aus-	ausbreiten	to spread out
bei-	beibringen	to teach (subject)
dar-	darstellen	to represent
davon-	davonlaufen	to run away
ein-	einstürzen	to collapse (building)
fern-	fernsehen	to watch tv
fort-	fortfahren	to continue; to go away
heim-	heimgehen	to go home
her-	hergeben	to hand over, give up
hin-	hinstellen	to put down
los-	losbrechen	to break out (riot etc.)
mit-	mitarbeiten	to co-operate
nach-	nachahmen	to imitate
nieder-	niedersinken	to sink down
statt-	stattfinden	to take place
teil-	teilnehmen	to take part
vor-	vorkommen	to seem; to happen
weiter-	weiterkommen	to progress
zu-	zugeben	to concede, admit
zurück-	zurückgeben	to give back

Note: *Her-, hin-* and *vor-* are often compounded with another prefix (e.g. *hinaus*gehen, *vorbei*fahren) and these compound prefixes remain *separable*.

Usage

1 When the verb is in the normal position, the prefix usually goes to the end of the clause or sentence.
     Ich *fing* um neun Uhr mit der Arbeit *an*.
     (I started work at nine o'clock.)
2 When the verb goes to the end of the sentence (see subordinat-

ing conjunctions on p. 88), the separable prefix is replaced on the front of the verb.

> Da ich um neun Uhr *an*fing, konnte ich um fünf Uhr nach Hause gehen.
>
> (As I began at nine o'clock, I could go home at five o'clock.)

3 When used in a past word, (past participle of perfect or pluperfect tense), the prefix is simply tacked on to the normal past word of the base verb (see points to watch 1, p. 49).

> Ich habe jeden Morgen um neun Uhr mit der Arbeit *ange*fangen.
>
> (I started work every morning at nine o'clock).

4 When using an infinitive, which always goes to the end, the prefix simply remains on the front of the infinitive.

> Ich mußte jeden Morgen um neun Uhr mit der Arbeit *anfangen*.
>
> (I had to start work every morning at nine o'clock.)

5 When used with *zu* + the infinitive, *zu* is sandwiched by the prefix and the base verb.

> Ich versuchte, immer um neun Uhr mit der Arbeit an*zu*fangen.
>
> (I always tried to start work at nine o'clock.

These rules apply to *all* separable prefixes.

Note: Remember to check for the base verb on the strong verb list (p. 70) when forming tenses of separable and inseparable verbs.

Exercises

A

Put the following separable verbs into the correct form of the present tense. Remember to check the base verb on the strong verb list and to place the prefix at the end.

1 Er (aufheben) das Buch vom Boden.
2 Ich (mitbringen) meinen besten Freund.
3 Die Kinder (fernsehen) gern.
4 Das alte Haus (niederbrennen).
5 Das Bild (darstellen) die Kindheit des Künstlers.

B

Put the verb in brackets into the correct form of the imperfect tense, then into the perfect tense.

1 Der Zug (vorbeifahren) so schnell wie der Blitz.
2 Er (zurückgeben) mir mein Buch.
3 Wir (wiedersehen) uns in London.
4 Wir (ankommen) abends um zehn Uhr in London.
5 Die Frauen (ausprobieren) das neue Auto.

Inseparable prefixes

As there are only nine of these, it is well worth learning them by heart.

be-	emp-	ent-	er-	
ge-	*hinter-	miß-	ver-	zer-

hinter is so rarely used separably that it is easier to consider it as inseparable.

The list on p. 58 sets out the most common inseparable verbs (verbs which have one of the above inseparable prefixes).

1 Weak inseparable verbs are shown by (wk) and rules for weak verbs apply (see sections on tenses pp 35-53).
2 Strong inseparable verbs are made up of a common strong verb as the base verb with the prefix added.

E.g. *sich befinden* has the base verb *finden*
begehen has the base verb *gehen*

3 To form the present and imperfect tenses, look at the strong verb list (pp 70-76) under the base verb, then simply add the prefix to the parts given.
4 To form the perfect tense see also perfect tense (p. 49, note 2).
5 All inseparable verbs have *haben* as their helping (auxiliary) verb (except *begegnen*, to meet, e.g. ich *bin* ihm begegnet).

Past Participle

Weak (wk)

Does not take *ge-* but ends in *-t*, and keeps inseparable prefix.

E.g. zerstören, zerstört (destroyed) from stören/ *ge*stört

gebrauchen, *gebraucht (needed) from brauchen/ *ge*braucht

} with *ge-* removed

*Note: the *ge-* here is the inseparable prefix.

Strong (most inseparables)

Does not take *ge-* but ends in *-en*, and keeps inseparable prefix.

E.g. beweisen, bewiesen (proved) from weisen/ *ge*wiesen

ertrinken, ertrunken (drowned) from trinken/ *ge*trunken

} with *ge-* removed

Some Common Inseparable Verbs

All these are strong unless indicated as weak.

Be- is often used together with other prefixes (e.g. *bee*influssen) but the compound prefix (*beein*) remains inseparable.

sich befinden	to be (situated; usually of objects, buildings etc.)
begehen	to commit (an offence)
begleiten (wk)	to accompany
begraben	to bury
begreifen	to grasp (idea, notion)
behalten	to keep (i.e. not give back)
sich benehmen	to behave
beschreiben	to describe
besitzen	to own, possess
besprechen	to discuss
bestätigen (wk)	to confirm
bestehen	to pass (exams)
bestehen auf (+ acc.)	to insist on
betreten	to walk/go into (e.g. ein Zimmer betreten)
beweisen	to prove, demonstrate

	empfangen	to receive (person, visitor)
	enthalten	to contain
	entlassen	to sack, dismiss
	entscheiden	to decide
	entsprechen (+ dat.)	to correspond to
	entstehen (aus + dat.)	to arise (out of)
sich	erbrechen	to be sick, vomit
	erfahren	to get to know, learn of
	erfinden	to invent
	erfüllen (wk)	to fill, to fulfil
	ergreifen	to grasp hold of, to grab
	erhalten	to receive
	erkennen	to recognize
	erklären (wk)	to explain
	erlauben (wk)	to allow
	ertragen	to put up with
	ertrinken	to drown
	erwachen (wk)	to wake up (self), awaken
	gebrauchen (wk)	to use
	gefallen (+ dat. of person)	to be pleasing (e.g. Es gefällt *mir*; I like it)
	gestehen	to admit, concede, confess
	hintergehen	to deceive
	hinterlassen	to leave, bequeath
	mißbrauchen (wk)	to misuse
	mißhandeln (wk)	to mishandle
	mißtrauen (wk)	to distrust
	verbinden	to link, associate
	verbrennen	to burn (something)
	verbringen	to spend (time)
sich	verfahren	to go wrong (when driving, travelling)
	verfallen	to fall into ruins
	vergeben	to forgive
	vergehen	to go by (of time)
	vergleichen	to compare
	vergraben	to bury (something)
	verkaufen (wk)	to sell
	verlassen	to leave (house, place)
	vermieten (wk)	to hire out
	verraten	to betray
sich	verraten	to give oneself away
	verschieben	to postpone, defer
	versehen	to equip, supply

59

versprechen	to promise
verstehen	to understand
verwenden	to use up
zerbrechen	to smash up
zerreißen	to rip to shreds
zerschneiden	to cut to pieces
zerstören (wk)	to destroy

Separable or inseparable

durch-	über-	um-	unter-	wider-	wieder-

These prefixes are used in both ways. The verbs must all be looked up in a dictionary to see whether they are separable or inseparable. Whether they are separable or not is absolutely vital to the meaning — you cannot simply decide which it will be!

E.g. *überlegen* (sep.) means 'to lay (something) over (something)'

Er *legte* sich eine Decke *über*.
(He covered himself with a blanket.)

überlegen (insep.) means 'to think about', 'to consider', 'to ponder'
Er *überlegte*, ob er ein neues Hemd kaufen sollte.
(He considered buying a new shirt.)

Here are just a few examples of verbs using these 'dual' prefixes. The abbreviation (str.) indicates a strong verb (see list pp 70-76) and (wk) indicates a weak verb (regular).

Separable		*Inseparable*	
*durch*fallen (str.)	to fail (exam)	*durch*bohren (wk)	to drill through
*über*fließen (str.)	to over- flow	*über*legen (wk)	to consider, think over

*um*steigen (str.)	to change (trains)	*umstellen* (wk)	to surround
*unter*gehen (str.)	to sink, decline	*unterbrechen* (str.)	to interrupt
*wider*spiegeln (wk)	to reflect, mirror	*widerstehen* (str.)	to resist
*wieder*geben (str.)	to give back	*wiederholen* (wk)	to repeat

Exercises

A

Using the Strong Verb List, give the correct form of the present tense and then of the imperfect for the following verbs:

1 Ich (begreifen)
2 Er (empfehlen)
3 Wir (beschreiben)
4 Mein Freund (brauchen)
5 Ich (empfangen)
6 Du (vergessen)
7 Ich (verschwinden)
8 Sie [you] (entscheiden)
9 Es (zerreißen)
10 Die Jungen (bestehen)

B

Put the verb in brackets into the imperfect tense.

1 Er (verstehen) den Befehl nicht.
2 Die Frau (verwenden) die Reste des Mittagessens für das Abendessen.
3 Der Verbrecher (gestehen) seine Schuld.
4 Zwei Tage später (erhalten) sie [they] den Brief.
5 Ich (beschließen), sofort nach Hause zu gehen.

Put the verbs in the following sentences into the perfect tense.

1 Er vergißt seinen Hut.
2 Der unartige Junge mißhandelt die Katze.
3 Das schöne Kleid gefällt mir gut.
4 Wir betreten leise den Wartesaal.
5 Der Direktor entläßt seine faule Sekretärin.

61

15 Subjunctive forms

sein and haben

	sein to be			*haben* to have	
	Pres.	Imperf.		Pres.	Imperf.
ich	sei	wäre	ich	habe	hätte
du	seist	wärest	du	habest	hättest
er	sei	wäre	er	habe	hätte
wir	seien	wären	wir	haben	hätten
ihr	seiet	wäret	ihr	habet	hättet
Sie	seien	wären	Sie	haben	hätten
sie	seien	währen	sie	haben	hätten

Other verbs

Present subjunctive

Take the stem of the verb, e.g. *lauf-* from laufen, to run. Add endings as italicised for the present subjunctive of *haben* in the table above. All verbs except *sein* follow this pattern. Note that the *ich* form has the same endings as the er form.

Imperfect subjunctive

Weak verbs: the form is exactly the same as for the normal imperfect tense (p. 39).
Strong verbs: the endings shown in the table above for imperfect tense are added to the imperfect tense er form as shown in the strong verb list (pp 72-76, column 4). Where the main vowel is 'a', 'o' or 'u' an umlaut ($\ddot{}$) is placed above that vowel.

Note: The few irregular imperfect subjunctives are: brennen, *brennte;* nennen, *nennte;* kennen, *kennte;* schwimmen, *schwömme;* helfen, *hülfe;* beginnen, *begönne;* denken, *dächte;* bringen, *brächte;* werfen, *würfe;* stehen, *stünde.* (All of these verbs appear on the strong verb list.)

Perfect subjunctive and pluperfect subjunctive

Both are formed by the normal method, except that the helping verb *haben* or *sein* is used in the present subjunctive for the perfect subjunctive tense and in the imperfect subjunctive for the pluperfect subjunctive tense.

Ich bin gekommen	becomes	Ich *sei* gekommen (perfect subjunctive)
Er hatte gesehen	becomes	Er *hätte* gesehen (pluperfect subjunctive)

Usage

The subjunctive is used for reported speech and also when dealing with a matter of opinion, something not proved or doubtful, e.g. after the verbs *denken, glauben.* The tense of the subjunctive is usually the tense which was originally used by the speaker, and does not always correspond to the tense used in English.

,Ich bin müde,' sagte der Mann.
('I am tired,' the man said.)

In reported speech this would be:

Der Mann sagte, daß er müde *sei.*
or
Der Mann sagte, er *sei* müde.
(The man said (that) he *was* tired.)

Note:
1 In German the present tense subjunctive is used, although the English form is *was.*
2 The word order is different when *daß* is not used.
3 The comma must be used at all times.
4 *Ich* in direct speech changes to *er* in reported speech in the example above.

63

5 Where the subjunctive form required looks the same as a normal present or perfect tense, then the next tense back in the past should be used.

E.g. They asked when I was returning home.
(The direct question is in the present tense: 'When *are* you *returning* home?'
Sie fragten, wann ich nach Hause zurück*ginge*.
(Zurück*gehe* is both normal present and subjunctive present, so to distinguish it as a subjunctive, the imperfect subjunctive is used.)

Wenn (if) plus subjunctive in a conditional sentence (applies to past tense only).

Note the use of tenses in the following examples. These sequences must be followed in *past tense* conditional sentences.
1 Wenn ich Zeit *hätte* [imperfect subjunctive], *würde* ich mit dir *kommen* [conditional].
(If I had time, I should come with you.)
(In the above *wenn* clause, the conditional tense could be used instead of the imperfect subjunctive, but this is clumsy and rarely used in written German.)
2 Wenn ich Zeit *gehabt hätte* [pluperfect subjunctive], *wäre* ich mit dir *gekommen* [pluperfect subjunctive].
(If I had had time, I should have come with you.)

Omission of *wenn*

Normally the *wenn* clause can be either first or second in the sentence. However, style allows *wenn* to be omitted from its clause, which must then be placed first in the sentence. Note the new position of the verb without *wenn*.

Hätte ich Zeit, dann würde ich mit dir kommen.
Hätte ich Zeit gehabt, so wäre ich mit dir gekommen.

Note here the addition of *so* or *dann* to the main clause when *wenn* is left out of the secondary clause.

64

16 Passive forms

present ⎱		
imperfect		
perfect	of *werden*	+PAST PARTICIPLE
pluperfect		(as used in normal perfect tense
future		(p. 48)
conditional ⎰		

Der Rasen *wird gemäht.* (present passive)
(The lawn is being mown.)
Bücher *wurden verkauft.* (imperfect passive)
(Books were being sold.)
Dieter *ist/war beraubt worden.* (perfect/pluperfect passive)
(Dieter has/had been robbed.)
Alles *wird/würde erklärt werden.* (future/conditional passive)
(Everything will/would be explained.)

Note: The perfect of *werden* is formed with *sein.*

Usage

The passive is used when the action done to something or someone is more important than the person or thing (known as the
agent) doing it.
   If the agent is to be included in a passive sentence, it is introduced by *von* and it is put into the dative case.
   Der Rasen wird *von* meinem Vater gemäht.
   (The lawn is being mown *by* my father.)

How to avoid the passive

Although using the passive voice improves style in written and
spoken German, it is nevertheless very often avoided.

Here are two common ways of avoiding the passive:

1 *Man* (meaning 'one', 'you', 'they', 'people')
By using *man*, as the subject of the sentence, the verb remains
in the normal active mood and *werden* is not used.
Man mäht den Rasen.
(The lawn is being mown.)

It can be seen in this and following examples that the subjects
of the examples used earlier have now become direct objects of
the sentences with *man*. Compare these with the examples at the
beginning of the chapter.

Man verkaufte Bücher.
(Books were being sold.)
Man hat/hatte Dieter beraubt.
(Dieter has/had been robbed.)
Man wird/würde alles erklären.
(Everything will/would be explained.)

The verbs whose past participles were used in the passive
sentences (*mähen*, gemäht; *verkaufen*, verkauft; *rauben*,
geraubt; *erklären*, erklärt) are now used in the ordinary
present, pluperfect, future and conditional tenses with *man* as
the subject.

2 Where an agent is mentioned in a passive sentence, it can be
used in a normal active sentence as the subject in the nominative
case.
Der Rasen wird von meinem Vater gemäht.
(The lawn is being mown by my father.)
becomes
Mein Vater mäht den Rasen.
(My father is mowing the lawn.)

Note: Past participles as adjective
The past participle is sometimes used as an adjective after the
present or imperfect tense of *sein* (to be). This is not a passive
form and simply describes the state of something.
Das Fenster ist/war *zerbrochen*.
(The window is/was broken, i.e. in a broken condition.)

The passive would be concerned with the act of breaking the
window.
Das Fenster *wurde* plötzlich *zerbrochen*.
(Suddenly the window was broken, i.e. someone broke it.)

Exercises

A

Complete the following present passive sentences by adding the correct form of the present tense of *werden*. (See *Sein, haben, werden,* p. 32).

1   Bier ____ hier sehr billig verkauft.
2   Die Karten ____ in der Eingangshalle ausgegeben.
3   Ich ____ immer vom Bahnhof abgeholt.
4   Der Mann ____ zur Polizeiwache begleitet.
5   Du ____ um acht Uhr erwartet.

B

Taking the same sentences, use *man* as the subject in rewriting them, thus avoiding the passive.

17   Position of the verb

Normal word order

The main verb stands in the second place in the sentence (i.e. not necessarily the second word but the second 'idea'). Any other verb or parts of verbs go to the end of the sentence.

Das Auto *ist* gestern gekommen.
(The car arrived yesterday.)
Das Auto, das Sie gekauft haben, *ist* gestern gekommen.
(The car which you bought arrived yesterday.)

(See also co-ordinating conjunctions p. 87).

Inverted word order

In direct questions the verb stands first, followed by the subject.

Ist das Auto gekommen?
(Has the car arrived?)

Note: If there is a 'question word' in the question, this precedes
the verb:

> Wann *ist* das Auto gekommen?
> (When did the car arrive?)

Transposed word order

Here the main verb moves right to the end of the clause. This
word order is used in relative clauses, subordinate clauses and
indirect questions. The verb in the main clause remains in the
normal place (second idea) if it is a statement.

1 Relative clause

Das Auto, mit dem Sie nach Köln fahren *wollen*, ist gestern
gekommen.
(The car in which you wish to travel to Cologne arrived yesterday.)

2 Subordinate clause

Das Auto ist gestern gekommen, weil Sie es für den falschen Tag
bestellt *haben*.
(The car arrived yesterday because you ordered it for the wrong
day.)
(See also p. 88 for full list of conjunctions which 'scare' the verb
to the end of the clause.)

3 Indirect question

Können Sie mir sagen, wann das Auto kommen *wird*?
(Can you tell me when the car will arrive?)

Note: When there is a double infinitive construction in transposed word order, the finite verb precedes the double infinitive
at the end of the clause.

> Das Auto, mit dem er nach Köln *hat* fahren wollen, ist gestern
> gekommen.
> (The car in which he wanted to travel to Cologne arrived
> yesterday.)

Summary

In stating that the verb in German is second in a sentence, the verb referred to is the verb in the main clause whose ending goes with the subject of the sentence. The subject and verb are not normally separated in a main clause. The subject occupies first position unless displaced, when it simply moves round the verb to third position, the verb being in second position.

Note: When a subordinate (secondary) clause (introduced by *wenn, als, weil, obwohl* etc.) begins a sentence, the whole clause is treated as the first element, the main verb is second and the subject third, as shown in this example:

Wenn ich Auto fahre (1) habe (2) ich (3) immer Angst.

An exception to the verb second rule is made in the case of simple questions.

Hast du Hunger? (Are you hungry?)
Willst du mit uns spielen? (Do you want to play with us?)

Here the simple question is formed by turning round the subject and verb.

Exercises

A

Rewrite the following sentences, putting the words in bold print at the beginning. Remember: verb second.

1 Paul hilft **seinem Vater** im Garten.
2 Wir fahren **jeden Tag*** in die Stadt.
3 **Um zwei Uhr*** ist die Mittagspause zu Ende.
4 Der Junge macht **die Schranktür** zu.
5 Wir kamen in das Zimmer, **als Herr Eber sprechen wollte.**

*Note: it is fairly common practice in German to begin a sentence with a time expression.

B

Put the following sentences into German, paying careful attention to the position of the verb.

1 Are you going to the cinema?
2 What do you want to eat?
3 On Sunday Johann and Michael were playing football.
4 If you don't mind, we're coming at four o'clock. (Wenn
   es dir egal ist, ...)
5 My mother always bought fruit in the supermarket.

18 Strong verb list

Listed here are the most common verbs which have a strong (or irregular) imperfect tense. All *three* tenses are given, in the er form. Where the present tense is regular (see p. 35), the form shown in the present tense column is marked *.

1 Auxiliary Verbs

(See sections on perfect, pluperfect, future and conditional pp 48-53 for their auxiliary usage.)

Infinitive	Meaning	Present Tense	Imperfect	Perfect Tense
haben	to have	hat	hatte	hat gehabt
sein	to be	ist	war	ist gewesen
werden	to become	wird	wurde	ist geworden

2 Modal Verbs

(Consult section on modal verbs, p 40, before using these.)

Infinitive	Meaning	Present Tense	Imperfect	Perfect Tense
dürfen	to be allowed	darf	durfte	This is rarely used. Use the
können	to be able	kann	konnte	past tense
mögen	may, to like	mag	mochte	(imperfect) instead.
müssen	must, to have to	muß	mußte	
sollen	to be to	soll	sollte	
wollen	to want to	will	wollte	
wissen*	to know	weiß	wußte	hat gewußt

*Although not a modal verb, wissen follows a similar pattern.

3 Mixed Verbs

In the imperfect tense the stem is strong (note vowel change) but the ending is weak. (See section on weak verbs, p. 39.)

Infinitive	Meaning	Present Tense	Imperfect	Perfect Tense
brennen	to burn	brennt*	brannte	hat gebrannt
bringen	to bring	bringt*	brachte	hat gebracht
denken	to think	denkt*	dachte	hat gedacht
kennen	to know	kennt*	kannte	hat gekannt
nennen	to name	nennt*	nannte	hat genannt
rennen	to run	rennt*	rannte	ist/hat gerannt
senden	to send	sendet*	sandte	hat gesandt
wenden	to turn	wendet*	wandte/ wendete	hat gewandt/ gewendet

*regular

4 Other common Strong Verbs

Infinitive	Meaning	Present Tense	Imperfect	Perfect Tense
backen	to bake	bäckt	buk/backte	hat gebacken
befehlen	to command	befiehlt	befahl	hat befohlen
beginnen	to begin	beginnt*	begann	hat begonnen
beißen	to bite	beißt*	biß	hat gebissen
bekommen	to get, obtain	bekommt*	bekam	hat bekommen
bersten	to burst	birst	barst	ist geborsten
bewegen	to induce	bewegt*	bewog	hat bewogen
biegen	to bend	biegt*	bog	hat gebogen
bieten	to offer	bietet*	bot	hat geboten
binden	to bind, tie	bindet*	band	hat gebunden
bitten	to ask, beg	bittet*	bat	hat gebeten
blasen	to blow	bläst	blies	hat geblasen
bleiben	to remain	bleibt*	blieb	ist geblieben
brechen	to break	bricht	brach	ist[+]/hat gebrochen
dringen	to pierce, penetrate	dringt*	drang	ist gedrungen
einladen	to invite	lädt ein	lud ein	hat eingeladen
empfehlen	to recommend	empfiehlt	empfahl	hat empfohlen
erlöschen	to die down, go out (of fire, light)	erlischt	erlosch	ist erloschen
erschrecken	to be frightened	erschrickt	erschrak	ist erschrocken
essen	to eat	ißt	aß	hat gegessen
fahren	to drive, ride	fährt	fuhr	ist gefahren
fallen	to fall	fällt	fiel	ist gefallen
fangen	to catch	fängt	fing	hat gefangen
finden	to find	findet*	fand	hat gefunden
fliegen	to fly	fliegt*	flog	ist geflogen

*regular
+to break through/out of (where motion is implied)

Infinitive	Meaning	Present Tense	Imperfect	Perfect Tense
fliehen	to flee	flieht*	floh	ist geflohen
fließen	to flow	fließt*	floß	ist geflossen
fressen	to eat	frißt	fraß	hat gefressen
frieren	to freeze	friert*	fror	hat gefroren
geben	to give	gibt	gab	hat gegeben
gehen	to go	geht*	ging	ist gegangen
gelingen	to succeed	gelingt*	gelang	ist gelungen
genießen	to enjoy	genießt*	genoß	hat genossen
geschehen	to happen	geschieht	geschah	ist geschehen
gewinnen	to gain, win	gewinnt*	gewann	hat gewonnen
gießen	to pour	gießt*	goß	hat gegossen
gleichen	to resemble	gleicht*	glich	hat geglichen
gleiten	to glide	gleitet*	glitt	ist geglitten
graben	to dig	gräbt	grub	hat gegraben
greifen	to seize	greift*	griff	hat gegriffen
halten	to hold, stop	hält	hielt	hat gehalten
hängen	to hang, be suspended	hängt*	hing	hat gehangen
heben	to lift	hebt*	hob	hat gehoben
heißen	to be called	heißt*	hieß	hat geheißen
helfen	to help	hilft	half	hat geholfen
klingen	to sound	klingt*	klang	hat geklungen
kommen	to come	kommt*	kam	ist gekommen
kriechen	to creep	kriecht*	kroch	ist gekrochen
laden	to load	lädt	lud	hat geladen
lassen	to let	läßt	ließ	hat gelassen
laufen	to run	läuft	lief	ist gelaufen
leiden	to suffer	leidet*	litt	hat gelitten
leihen	to lend	leiht*	lieh	hat geliehen
lesen	to read	liest	las	hat gelesen
liegen	to lie	liegt*	lag	hat gelegen
lügen	to tell lies	lügt*	log	hat gelogen
meiden	to avoid	meidet*	mied	hat gemieden
messen	to measure	mißt	maß	hat gemessen

*regular

73

Infinitive	Meaning	Present Tense	Imperfect	Perfect Tense
nehmen	to take	nimmt	nahm	hat genommen
pfeifen	to whistle	pfeift*	pfiff	hat gepfiffen
preisen	to praise	preist*	pries	hat gepriesen
raten	to advise; guess	rät	riet	hat geraten
reiben	to rub	reibt*	rieb	hat gerieben
reißen	to tear	reißt*	riß	hat gerissen
reiten	to ride	reitet*	ritt	ist+/hat geritten
riechen	to smell	riecht*	roch	hat gerochen
rufen	to call	ruft*	rief	hat gerufen
scheiden	to part	scheidet*	schied	ist geschieden
scheinen	to appear; shine	scheint*	schien	hat geschienen
schieben	to shove, push	schiebt*	schob	hat geschoben
schießen	to shoot	schießt*	schoß	hat geschossen
schlafen	to sleep	schläft	schlief	hat geschlafen
schlagen	to strike, hit	schlägt	schlug	hat geschlagen
schleichen	to creep	schleicht*	schlich	ist geschlichen
schließen	to shut	schließt*	schloß	hat geschlossen
schmelzen	to melt	schmilzt	schmolz	ist geschmolzen
schneiden	to cut	schneidet*	schnitt	hat geschnitten
schreiben	to write	schreibt*	schrieb	hat geschrieben
schreien	to cry out, shout	schreit*	schrie	hat geschrien
schreiten	to stride	schreitet	schritt	ist geschritten
schweigen	to be silent	schweigt*	schwieg	hat geschwiegen
schwellen	to swell	schwillt	schwoll	ist geschwollen

*regular
+where motion is implied use *sein*

Infinitive	Meaning	Present Tense	Imperfect	Perfect Tense
schwimmen	to swim	schwimmt*	schwamm	ist geschwommen
schwingen	to swing	schwingt*	schwang	hat geschwungen
schwören	to swear	schwört*	schwor	hat geschworen
sehen	to see	sieht	sah	hat gesehen
singen	to sing	singt*	sang	hat gesungen
sinken	to sink	sinkt*	sank	ist gesunken
sitzen	to sit	sitzt	saß	hat gesessen
spinnen	to spin	spinnt*	spann	hat gesponnen
sprechen	to speak	spricht	sprach	hat gesprochen
springen	to spring, jump	springt*	sprang	ist gesprungen
stechen	to prick, sting	sticht	stach	hat gestochen
stehen	to stand	steht*	stand	hat gestanden
stehlen	to steal	stiehlt	stahl	hat gestohlen
steigen	to ascend	steigt*	stieg	ist gestiegen
sterben	to die	stirbt	starb	ist gestorben
stoßen	to push, knock, bump	stößt	stieß	hat gestoßen
streichen	to paint, spread [butter]	streicht*	strich	hat gestrichen
streiten	to argue	streitet*	stritt	hat gestritten
tragen	to carry, wear	trägt	trug	hat getragen
treffen	to hit, meet	trifft	traf	hat getroffen
treiben	to drive	treibt*	trieb	hat getrieben
treten	to step, kick[football]	tritt	trat	ist[+]/hat getreten
trinken	to drink	trinkt*	trank	hat getrunken

*regular
[+]where motion into is implied use *sein* (e.g. Er *ist* ins Zimmer getreten.)

75

Infinitive	Meaning	Present Tense	Imperfect	Perfect Tense
tun	to do	tut*	tat	hat getan
verbieten	to forbid	verbietet*	verbot	hat verboten
verderben	to spoil	verdirbt	verdarb	hat verdorben
vergessen	to forget	vergißt	vergaß	hat vergessen
verlieren	to lose	verliert*	verlor	hat verloren
ver- schwinden	to disap- pear	ver- schwindet*	verschwand	ist ver- schwunden
verzeihen	to pardon	verzeiht*	verzieh	hat verziehen
wachsen	to grow	wächst	wuchs	ist gewachsen
waschen	to wash	wäscht	wusch	hat gewaschen
weisen	to show	weist*	wies	hat gewiesen
werfen	to throw	wirft	warf	hat geworfen
wiegen	to weigh	wiegt*	wog	hat gewogen
winden	to wind	windet*	wand	hat gewunden
ziehen	to draw, pull	zieht*	zog	hat gezogen
zwingen	to force	zwingt*	zwang	hat ge- zwungen

*regular

English/German Reference List of STRONG VERBS only

(Common verbs not included in this list are weak, unless they are compounds of strong verbs.) The numbers beside certain verbs refer you to one of the first three special sections on the German strong verb list, p. 70.

advise	raten	bake	backen
argue	streiten	be	sein[1]
appear	scheinen	be able to	können[2]
ascend	steigen	be called	heißen
ask	fragen	be frightened	erschrecken
avoid	meiden	be quiet, silent	schweigen

be sitting	sitzen	forget	vergessen
be to	sollen[2]	forgive	verzeihen
become	werden[1]	freeze	frieren
beg, ask	bitten	gain	gewinnen
begin	beginnen	get	bekommen
bend	biegen	give	geben
bind	binden	glide	gleiten
bite	beißen	go (on foot)	gehen
blow	blasen	go (by tran-	
break	brechen	sport)	fahren
bring	bringen[3]	go out (of	
burn	brennen[3]	fire)	erlöschen
burst	bersten	go up	steigen
call, name	nennen	grab	greifen
call, shout	rufen	grow	wachsen
called (see 'be called')		guess	raten
can (see 'be able')		halt	halten
carry	tragen	hang	hängen
catch	fangen	happen	geschehen
climb	steigen	have	haben[1]
close	schließen	have to	müssen[2]
come	kommen	help	helfen
command	befehlen	hit (strike a	
creep	kriechen,	blow)	schlagen
	schleichen	hit (target)	treffen
cry out	schreien	hold	halten
cut	schneiden	induce	bewegen
die	sterben	invite	einladen
dig	graben	jump	springen
drink	trinken	kick	stoßen
drive	treiben	know (person)	kennen[3]
(animals)		know (fact)	wissen[2]
drive (car, etc.)	fahren	lend	leihen
do	tun	let	lassen
eat	essen	lie (tell lies)	lügen
eat (of		lie (be lying)	
animals)	fressen	down)	liegen
enjoy	genießen	lift	heben
fall	fallen	like to	mögen[2]
find	finden	load	laden
flee	fliehen	lose	verlieren
flow	fließen	may	dürfen[2]
force	zwingen	measure	messen

meet	treffen	shout	rufen
melt	schmelzen	shove	stoßen
must	müssen[2]	show	weisen
name	nennen[3]	shut	schließen
obtain	bekommen	silent (see 'be silent')	
offer	bieten	sing	singen
order,		sink	sinken
command	befehlen	sit (be sitting)	sitzen
ought (see 'be to', past tense)		sleep	schlafen
pace	schreiten	smell	riechen
pardon	verzeihen	smell (nice)	riechen
part	scheiden	smell (nasty)	stinken
praise	preisen	sound	klingen
press (of		speak	sprechen
crowd)	dringen	spin	spinnen
prick	stechen	spoil	verderben
pour	gießen	spring	springen
pull	ziehen	stand	stehen
push	schieben,	start	beginnen
	stoßen	stay	bleiben
quiet (see 'be quiet')		steal	stehlen
read	lesen	step	treten,
recommend	empfehlen		schreiten
remain	bleiben	sting	stechen
resemble	gleichen	stop	halten
ride (horse)	reiten	stride	schreiten
ride (bike etc.)	fahren	strike	schlagen
rip	reißen	stroke	streichen
run	laufen, rennen	suffer	leiden
run (of water)	fließen	swear	schwören
run away	fliehen	swell	schwellen
rub	reiben	swim	schwimmen
score (goal)	(ein Tor)	swing	schwingen
	schießen	take	nehmen
scream	schreien	talk	sprechen
see	sehen	tear	reißen
seem	scheinen	tell lies	lügen
seize	greifen	think	denken[3]
send	senden[3]	throw	werfen
separate	scheiden	tie	binden
shine	scheinen	turn (left	
shoot	schießen	etc.)	biegen
should (see 'be to', past tense)		turn (to)	wenden[3]

78

vanish	verschwinden	weigh	wiegen
walk	gehen	whistle	pfeifen
want	wollen[2]	win	gewinnen
wash	waschen	wind	winden
wear	tragen	write	schreiben

Part IV

19 Adverbs

Apart from the following list of common adverbs, a large number of basic adjectives may be used adverbially.

E.g. Ein Expreß ist ein schneller Zug (adjective = fast)
Ein Expreß fährt schnell (adverb = fast, quickly)

Common adverbs

also (then, therefore, so)
Wir kamen *also* nach Hause.
(So we came home.)

damals (then, at that time)
Im 18. Jahrhundert gab es viele Krankheiten. *Damals* war die Kindersterblichkeit sehr hoch.
(There was much disease in the 18th century. At that time infant mortality was very high.)

dann (then, next)
Wir tranken unseren Kaffee und *dann* gingen wir weiter.
(We drank our coffee and then we carried on.)

auch (also, too)
Er mußte *auch* seine Mahlzeiten selbst zubereiten.
(He also had to prepare his own meals.)

bald (soon)
Bald ging die Sonne unter.
(Soon the sun set.)

doch (however, but, yet; also used emphatically)
Ich kann *doch* schwimmen
(But I *can* swim.)

Er konnte nicht schwimmen, *doch* kam er mit ins Hallenbad.
(He couldn't swim, yet he came to the baths with us.)

eben (just, exactly)
Das wollte ich *eben* sagen.
(That's what I was just going to say.)

Eben das wollte ich sagen.
(That's exactly what I was going to say.)

gerade (just) (used like *eben*)

erst (not until)
Der Direktor kam *erst* um zehn Uhr.
(The boss didn't arrive until ten o'clock.)

fast (almost)
Ich schlief *fast* ein.
(I almost fell asleep.)

ganz (quite, completely)
Die junge Dame wurde *ganz* rot.
(The young lady went quite red.)

gar, überhaupt (at all)
Ich wollte *gar* nicht warten.
(I did not want to wait at all.)

gern (shows liking)
Kinder essen *gern* Bonbons.
(Children like (eating) sweets.)

genug (enough; note position as in English)
Es war nicht stark *genug*.
(It was not strong enough.)

immer (always, still)
Er kommt *immer* um zehn Uhr.
(He always comes at ten o'clock.)

Löhne und Preise steigen *immer* höher.
(Wages and prices are rising still higher.)

jetzt (now)
Jetzt müssen wir das Rad wechseln.
(We have to change the wheel now.)

nun (now) Used like *jetzt* and also in such expressions as *Nun also!*; Well, now!

kaum (hardly)
Der Feuerwehrmann konnte *kaum* atmen.
(The fireman could hardly breathe.)

81

lange (for a long time)
Der Wagen stand *lange* vor der Garage.
(The car stood outside the garage for a long time.)

leider (unfortunately)
Die Flut stieg *leider* zu hoch.
(Unfortunately the tide rose too high.)

nicht (not)
Der Bus kam *nicht*.
(The bus did not come.)

nicht mehr (no longer)
Ich konnte es *nicht mehr* ertragen.
(I could put up with it no longer.)

nie (never)
Sie hatte ihn *nie* in ihrem Leben gesehen.
(She had never seen him before in her life.)

noch (yet, still)
Wir haben *noch* Zeit.
(We still have time.)

noch nicht (not yet)
Das habe ich *noch nicht* verstanden.
(I have not yet understood that.)

nur (only)
Ich wollte *nur* schlafen.
(I only wanted to sleep.)

oft (often)
Er war *oft* in Frankreich.
(He often went to France.)

plötzlich (suddenly)
Plötzlich fiel sie hin.
(She suddenly collapsed.)

schon (already)
Es regnet *schon*.
(It is already raining.)

sehr (very, very much)
Er liebte sie *sehr*.
(He loved her very much.)

Es war *sehr* warm.
(It was very warm.)

sofort (immediately)
Der Polizist stieg *sofort* aus seinem Wagen aus.
(The policeman got out of his car immediately.)

sogar (even)
Er wollte *sogar* für mich zahlen.
(He even wanted to pay for me.)

vielleicht (perhaps)
Kommen Sie *vielleicht* morgen?
(Perhaps you'll come tomorrow, will you?)

wieder (back, again)
Die Kinder gingen *wieder* ins Bett.
(The children went back to bed.)

ziemlich (rather)
Der Preis war *ziemlich* hoch.
(The price was rather high.)

Adverbs from Adjectives

These are the commonest adjectives used as adverbs:

schnell	fast (adj.), quickly (adv.)
gut	good (adj.), well (adv.)
langsam	slow (adj.), slowly (adv.)
spät	late (adj. + adv.)
früh	early (adj. + adv.)
einfach	simple (adj.), simply (adv.)
leicht	light, easy (adj.), lightly, easily (adv.)
vollkommen	complete (adj.), completely (adv.)

Position of the adverb in German

The adverb normally *relates to a verb*, and it is placed as near to that verb as possible.

Study the position of the adverb here:

Er *las schnell* den Brief von seinem Onkel.
Er wollte den Brief von seinem Onkel *schnell lesen.*

When the adverb *relates to an adjective*, it is placed immediately
before that adjective.

Der Direktor nahm den Fehler *sehr ernst.*
In England wird die Wirtschaftslage *noch schlimmer* als in
Deutschland.

(Note the exception of 'genug': (See list p. 81).

Exercises

A

The adverb in each of the following sentences has been given in
English. Use the list on pp 80-83 to find the correct German for
each one and rewrite the sentences in full.

1 Hans fühlte sich (suddenly) wohl.
2 Sie gingen (next) in die Apotheke.
3 Das Schiff war (soon) unterwegs nach Amerika.
4 Mein Bruder las (often) im Bett.
5 Er war (almost) so groß wie ich.
6 Die Zeitungen kommen (always) um sieben Uhr morgens.
7 Vater spielte (never) Fußball mit uns.
8 Meine Mutter war (at that time) ziemlich glücklich.
9 Karin aß (only) Süßigkeiten.
10 Sie blieben nicht (for long).

B

Put the adverb (given in English) into German and use it in the
sentence which it follows.

1 Wir konnten durch den Nebel sehen. (not)
2 Das wollte er sagen. (just)
3 Sie ging in das Lebensmittelgeschäft. (so)
4 Er aß ein Ei zum Frühstück. (always)
5 Die Augen fielen mir zu. (almost)

20 Comparative and superlative of adverbs and adjectives

In English the -er/-est endings are usually used with short adjectives, while the more/most combination is mostly used with long adjectives and nearly all adverbs.

Basic	Comparative	Superlative
big	bigger	biggest
economically	more economically	most economically

In German the adjective or adverb takes -er and -st (-est when the basic adjective/adverb ends in -s, -sch, -ß, -z, -t or -d).

Basic	Comparative	Superlative
schnell	schneller	der (das, die) schnellste (adj) am schnellsten (adv)
schlecht	schlechter	der (das, die) schlechteste (adj) am schlechtesten (adv)

All of the following single-syllable adjectives whose main vowel is a, o or u take an umlaut (ä, ö, ü) in the comparative and superlative, and the pattern for them is as follows:

warm	wärmer	der (das, die) wärmste (adj) am wärmsten (adv)

Alt, arg, arm, dumm, grob, hart, jung, kalt, klug, krank, kurz, lang, scharf, stark, schwach, schwarz. Also -oft (adv.).

A few common adjectives/adverbs are irregular:

groß	größer	der (das, die) größte/
		am größten
gut	besser	der (das, die) beste/
		am besten
hoch*	höher	der (das, die) höchste/
		am höchsten
nah	näher	der (das, die) nächste/
		am nächsten
viel	mehr	der (das, die) meiste/
		am meisten
viele	mehr	die meisten (plural)/
		am meisten

*When placed before its noun, hoch becomes hoh, e.g. das hohe Gebäude (the tall building).

The usage of superlative forms

der, das, die -ste/am -sten

When the *superlative of an adverb* is needed, use *am -sten.*

Wie komme ich *am besten* zum Bahnhof?
(What is the best way to the station?)

(Note: the German adverb in this case is rendered by the adjective in English.)

When the *superlative of an adjective* is needed and the *noun it describes is used or understood,* use *der, das, die -ste,* (normal adjective endings as on case table p 21).

Dieses Buch ist gut, aber das ist *das beste* (Buch).
(This book is good, but that one is the best.)

Otherwise use *am -sten.* (This form is always the same.)

Milch ist gut, Limonade ist auch gut, aber Kaffee ist *am besten.*
(Milk is good, lemonade is good too, but coffee is the best.)

86

21 Conjunctions

Conjunctions are words used to join two sentences together.

Co-ordinating conjunctions

These do not affect normal word order.

und	and
aber	but (in the sense of 'however')
oder	or
denn	for, as
sondern	but (in the sense of 'on the contrary')

Note the difference between *aber* and *sondern*.

aber, but (however)
    Not rich, *but* happy (He is not rich, however he is happy.)
    Er ist nicht reich, *aber* er ist glücklich.
sondern, but (on the contrary)
    Not rich but poor (He is not rich, on the contrary he is poor.)
    Er ist nicht reich, *sondern* er ist arm.

Examples

Notice how two sentences are joined by one of these
conjunctions and that *the position of the verb is not affected*.

1   Er ist im Wohnzimmer. Er liest die Zeitung.
     Er ist im Wohnzimmer *und* er liest die Zeitung.
2   Er bleibt zu Hause. Es regnet.
     Er bleibt zu Hause, *denn* es regnet.
3   Jeden Tag kam er spät nach Hause. Immer brachte er etwas
      mit.
     Jeden Tag kam er spät nach Hause, *aber* immer brachte er
      etwas mit.

Exercises

A

Join the pairs of sentences together, using the conjunction suggested in brackets.

1 Johann spielte im Garten. Maria spielte mit. (und)
2 Hans wollte nicht arbeiten. Er wollte spielen. (sondern)
3 Ich war nicht hungrig. Mein Bruder gab mir ein Käsebrot. (aber)
4 Wir konnten nicht schwimmen. Das Wasser war zu kalt. (denn)
5 Du gehst allein nach Hause. Wir kommen alle mit. (oder)

B

Choose the most suitable conjunction to join the following pairs of sentences.

1 Der Lehrer war sehr alt. Er konnte sehr gut hören.
2 Mein Auto fährt nicht so gut. Der Vergaser geht kaputt.
3 Dieser Rock ist zu teuer. Ich mag ihn auch nicht.
4 Die Mädchen sollen mitkommen. Ich komme nicht mit.
5 Der Direktor der großen Firma sucht eine Sekretärin. Viele Mädchen bewerben sich um die Stelle.
6 Ich kam nicht zu spät an. Ich kam zehn Minuten zu früh an.
7 Heinrichs Tante ist ganz jung. Sie ist total humorlos.
8 Mein Beruf ist sehr interessant. Ich verdiene nicht viel Geld.
9 Der Kellner brachte mir kein Fleisch. Er legte ein großes Stück Fisch auf meinen Teller.
10 Der unartige Junge hatte sein Deutschheft nicht dabei. Er vergaß immer alles.

Subordinating conjunctions

There are several subordinating conjunctions, of which these are the most common:

bis	until
ehe, bevor	before
während	while
indem	by (doing something); while

nachdem	after
seitdem	since (time)
da, weil	since, because
daß	that
so daß	so that, with the result that
im Falle daß, falls	in case that
damit	in order that, so that
wenn	if, when, whenever
selbst wenn, auch wenn, wenn auch	even if
als ob, als wenn	as if
ob	whether, if (in indirect questions)
als	when, as
wann	when (in indirect questions)
wie	how, as
obwohl, obgleich, obschon, obzwar	although
sobald/sowie	as soon as
sooft	as often as
solange	as long as

All of these *send the verb to the end* of the clause which they introduce (see transposed word order, p 68).

Examples

1 Wir gingen in die Stadt. Es *regnete* stark.
Wir gingen in die Stadt, *obgleich* es stark *regnete*.
2 Erich wollte nicht hinausgehen. Walter *war* auf der Straße.
Erich wollte nicht hinausgehen, *weil* Walter auf der Straße *war*.
3 Ich kam ins Zimmer. Alle Leute *waren* da.
Ich kam ins Zimmer, *bevor* alle Leute da *waren*.

When a subordinate clause comes first, the subject and verb of the main clause are reversed.

Obgleich es stark *regnete, gingen wir* in die Stadt.
Weil Walter auf der Straße *war, wollte Erich* nicht hinausgehen.
Bevor alle Leute da *waren, kam ich* ins Zimmer.

(See also position of the verb, p 67).

Exercises

A

Supply the German conjunction for the meaning given. Write out the whole sentence.

1 Er sah seinen Onkel, (when) er in das Wohnzimmer kam.
2 (After) ich aus meinem Auto gestiegen war, sah ich meine Uhr an.
3 Der Film läuft heute nicht, (because) heute der erste Weihnachtstag ist.
4 (As) du siehst, kann er sein Fahrrad nicht reparieren.
5 Er bemerkte, (that) sein rechter Schuh ein Loch hatte.
6 (Although) wir nicht viel Geld hatten, gingen wir ins Kino.
7 (Before) ich hierher kam, war ich in London.
8 Herr Wingertaler fragte, (whether) er nach Hause gehen könnte.
9 (Whenever) ich ohne Regenschirm komme, regnet es immer in Strömen.
10 Das Kind mußte sich die Hände waschen, (before) es essen durfte.

B

Join the following sentences with a suitable subordinating conjunction from the following list: als (or weil), bevor, daß obgleich, wenn. Each is to be used once only. Remember the rule about verb position.

1 Die zwei Damen saßen unter dem Baum. Das Gras war sehr naß.
2 Viele Kinder spielten mit einem Ball. Ihre Mütter riefen sie zu sich nach Hause.
3 Der Briefträger bringt die Briefe nie ins Haus. Er sieht das Schild ,Bissiger Hund!'
4 Die Katze lief weg. Sie sah den bösen Hund von nebenan.
5 Er sah. Ich hatte Schwierigkeiten.

90

22 Relative pronouns

A relative pronoun in English is the word **who, whom, whose** or **which**, referring back to a noun in the same sentence.

The boy **whom** I saw is his brother.

In German, the idea is exactly the same.

Der Junge, *den* ich sah, ist sein Bruder.

	Nom. (subject)	Acc. (dir. obj.)	Dat. (ind. obj.) to/for	*Gen. whose
masculine	der	den	dem	dessen
neuter	das	das	dem	dessen
feminine	die	die	der	deren
plural	die	die	denen	deren

Forms of the word *welcher* may be met with as relative pronouns instead of the words above, but those shown in the table are more common and you should learn to use them.

Apart from *denen* (dative plural), all relative pronouns take exactly the same form as the *der, das, die* words in the nominative, accusative and dative shown in the Declension Table (p 21).

*For special note on genitive whose (last column above), see special genitive section (p 92).

Usage of the relative pronoun

Look at the table above. The choice of the pronoun (from the first three in each line across) to be used depends on the job or function of the word *who, whom* or *which* in the relative clause.

In the following examples, the relative pronoun in bold or italic type, refers back to a masculine noun.

1 Der Mann, der (subject) im Auto sitzt, ist mein Vater.
  The man *who* (subject) is sitting in the car is my father.
2 Der Mann, den (direct object) du meinst, ist im Auto.
  The man *whom* (direct object) you mean is in the car.
3 Ich sehe den Mann, dem (indirect object) er das Geld gab.
  I can see the man *to whom* (indirect object) he gave the money.

In the examples above, the masculine relative pronoun has been used in the subject, direct object and indirect object forms as shown on the table on pp 91, because the relative pronoun refers back in each case to *Mann*, a masculine word.

If a neuter or feminine noun (instead of *der Mann*) had been used, a form of the neuter relative pronoun (*das, das, dem*) or of the feminine relative pronoun (*die, die, der*) would have been used.

If a plural noun (instead of *der Mann*) had been used, a form of the plural relative pronoun (*die, die, denen*) would have been used.

The genitive relative pronoun

Masculine and neuter	Feminine and plural	English
dessen	deren	whose, of which

If the thing or person belongs to a male person or a masculine or neuter noun, use dessen.

Herr Schmidt, dessen Frau ich kenne, wohnt hier.
Die Dame kaufte das Bild, dessen Glas zerbrochen war.

If the thing or person belongs to a female person or a feminine or plural noun, use deren.

Die Kinder, deren Mutter hier arbeitet, spielen dort drüben.
Die Frau, deren Mann ich kenne, wohnt hier.

Use of prepositions in a relative clause

When prepositions are used before a relative pronoun, the relative pronoun should be in the form or case (accusative or dative) which the preposition demands. (See section on prepositions which always take the accusative, (p 10) and dative, (p 16) or either, depending on motion or position (pp 114-118).

Here are some examples: the relative pronoun is in italic type and the noun it refers back to is repeated in brackets in the nominative case.

1 Ich suchte einen Bleistift, mit *dem* ich zeichnen konnte.
   (der Bleistift)
   (I was looking for a pencil with which I could draw.)
   (I was looking for a pencil to draw with.)
2 Das ist das Kino, in *das* ich oft als Junge ging. (das Kino)
   (That is the cinema I often went to as a boy.)
3 Das Haus, vor *dem* das Auto steht, gehört meiner Tante.
   (das Haus)
   (The house in front of which the car is standing belongs to my aunt.)
   (The house the car is standing in front of belongs to my aunt.)

German makes us use a relative pronoun where English often seems to avoid it. Look again at the translations of the above sentences. *Do not try to avoid the use of the relative pronoun in German.*

'The lady sitting in the waiting room' in German would be: *Die Dame, die* im Wartesaal *sitzt/saß.*

Word order with relative pronouns

1 The *noun referred to* is usually the *last thing before a comma* (see 1 in the examples below).
2 The *relative pronoun* is always *first after that comma,* placed as closely as possible to the noun it relates to (sometimes with a preposition before it — see previous section). See 2 in the examples below.
3 The *verb* in the *relative clause* is always *last* in that clause (followed by a comma or full stop). See 3 in the examples below.

Der Junge sah *den Mann* (1), *der* (2) ihm Bonbons *gab* (3).

Der Junge (1), *den* (2) ich *kenne* (3), wohnt in Berlin.

A relative clause always begins with a relative pronoun and ends with a verb.

Exercises

A

In the following sentences the noun referred back to is the subject of the relative clause. Supply the correct form of the relative pronoun (subject/nominative case) in each one.

1 Der Mann, d____ auf der Bank sitzt, ißt seine Butterbrote.
2 Sie kannten die Jungen, d____ das Fenster zerbrachen.
3 Das Buch lag auf dem Tisch, d____ im Wohnzimmer stand.
4 Er gab das Buch der Frau, d____ an der Kasse war.
5 Wir kauften uns das Pferd, d____ uns gefallen hatte.

B

The same must be done in these sentences, but the relative pronoun is now the direct object in its clause so the accusative form must be used.

1 Die zwei Kinder, d____ wir gestern sahen, waren sehr übermütig.
2 Der Tisch, d____ ich kaufen wollte, war zu teuer.
3 Der Zollbeamte fand die Flasche Schnaps, d____ der Reisende vor ihm versteckt hatte.
4 Hans arbeitete schwer in dem Garten, d____ er von seinem Vater bekommen hatte.
5 Ich mußte für das Buch, d____ ich lesen wollte, viel Geld bezahlen.

C

Now the relative pronoun is to be used in the dative case.

1 Der Mann, d____ der Kunde das sagte, ist nicht mehr da.
2 Paul wollte seine Freunde suchen, mit d____ er oft spielte.
3 Das ist die Familie, bei d____ wir fünf Wochen blieben.
4 Ich meldete dem Polizisten, mit d____ du gestern gesprochen hast, den Unfall.
5 Die ältere Dame, d____ er alles gab, war seine Frau.

D

Here the genitive forms *dessen* or *deren* must be used.

1 Der alte Mann schimpfte die Jungen, d____ Ball in seinem Garten lag.

2 Es ist gefährlich mit einem Auto zu fahren, d——
Reifen abgenutzt sind.
3 Frau Weber, d—— Auto auf der Straße steht, ist in der
Bank.
4 In dem Haus, d—— Fenster zerbrochen sind, schläft ein
Landstreicher.
5 Der Zug, d —— Wagen ganz neu sind, fährt schnell am
Bahnhof vorbei.

E

Join the following sentences making the second one of each
pair into a relative clause by turning the bracketed element
into the appropriate relative pronoun. (Remember: verb
to the end.)

1 Vor dem Kino war eine Schlange Leute. (Sie) hatten
schon stundenlang gewartet.
2 Nach dem Abendessen las ich das Buch. Ich fand (es) auf
dem Lehnstuhl.
3 Der Politiker hielt seine Rede. Er hatte (sie) am Tage
vorher ausgearbeitet.
4 Wir flogen mit demselben Flugzeug. Wir flogen letztes
Jahr (damit).
5 Frau Weber fand ihre Handtasche. Sie hatte (sie) im
Supermarkt verloren.

23 Numerals, dates and time

Numbers

1	eins	1st	erste
2	zwei	2nd	zweite
3	drei	3rd	dritte
4	vier	4th	vierte
5	fünf	5th	fünfte
6	sechs	6th	sechste
7	sieben	7th	sieb(en)te
8	acht	8th	achte
9	neun	9th	neunte
10	zehn	10th	zehnte

11	elf	11th	elfte
12	zwölf	12th	zwölfte
13	dreizehn	13th	dreizehnte
14	vierzehn	14th	vierzehnte
15	fünfzehn	15th	fünfzehnte
16	sechzehn	16th	sechzehnte
17	siebzehn	17th	siebzehnte
18	achtzehn	18th	achtzehnte
19	neunzehn	19th	neunzehnte
20	zwanzig	20th	zwanzig*ste*
21	*ein*und*zwanzig*	21st	einundzwanzig*ste*
etc			
30	dreißig	30th	dreißig*ste*
40	vierzig	40th	vierzigste
50	fünfzig	50th	fünfzigste
60	sechzig	60th	sechzigste
70	siebzig	70th	siebzigste
80	achtzig	80th	achtzigste
90	neunzig	90th	neunzigste
100	hundert	100th	hundert*ste*
1,000	tausend	1,000th	tausend*ste*

Note also :

ein Hundert	Hunderte (hundreds)
ein Tausend	Tausende (thousands)
eine Million	Millionen (millions)

1 *Zum ersten, zweiten, dritten Mal:* for the first, second, third time.

E.g. Ich komme zum ersten Mal nach Deutschland.
(It's the first time I've been to Germany.)

2 Er ist der *E*rste.
(He is the first.)
The number has a capital letter if standing alone.

3 Numbers between 20 and 100: the units are always said and written first and are joined by *und*, e.g. 84 = vier*und*achtzig.

4 All numbers over 21 are simply strung together in one word but still using *und* at the end as shown in note 3, e.g. 2984 = zweitausendneunhundertvier*und*achtzig.

5 *erste, zweite, dritte* etc. take normal adjective endings as after *der, das, die.*

Dates

Die Wochentage	Die Monate		Die Vier Jahreszeiten
Montag	Januar	Juli	der Frühling
Dienstag	Februar	August	der Sommer
Mittwoch	März	September	der Herbst
Donnerstag	April	Oktober	der Winter
Freitag	Mai	November	(*Im* Frühling
Samstag (Sonna-bend)	Juni	Dezember	*In* spring etc)
Sonntag			

der Tag (-e)   der Monat (-e)   das Jahr (-e)

Der wievielte ist heute?
Den wievielten haben wir heute? } What is the date today?

Heute *ist der* 21. (einundzwanzigste) Juli.   Today is
Heute *haben* wir *den* 21. (einundzwanzigsten) Juli.   21st July.

At the head of a letter etc. this date would always be written:
Berlin, *den* 21. Juli

Time

... o'clock	... Uhr
three o'clock	drei Uhr
... (minutes) to ...	... (Minuten) vor ...
twenty to eight	zwanzig (Minuten) vor acht
... (minutes) past ...	... (Minuten) nach ...
five past ten	fünf (Minuten) nach zehn
quarter to/quarter past	Viertel vor/Viertel nach
quarter to nine	Viertel vor neun, fünfzehn
	Minuten vor neun

half past
In German this is seen as half the next hour (i.e. halfway to the next hour)

half past one (add one)	halb zwei
half past eight (add one)	halb neun
half past twelve (add one)	halb eins

Additional expressions used in time-telling

morgens	in the morning
mittags	at midday
nachmittags	in the afternoon
abends	in the evening
nachts	at night
fünf Uhr morgens	five o'clock in the morning
neun Uhr abends	nine o'clock in the evening

24 Notes on noun genders and plurals

Although there are no fixed and infallible rules governing the gender and plural of nouns, these are some useful guidelines which can be followed to give a general impression of the patterns of plurals and genders which exist.

masculine nouns

These should always be looked up and learned. There are no reliable rules governing this group. (However, see section on weak masculine and adjectival nouns, p 99.)

neuter nouns

Nouns ending in *-ium*, *-chen* and *-lein* are always neuter. The ending *-ium* changes to *-ien* in the plural. The endings *-chen* and *-lein* remain unchanged in the plural.

Singular	*Plural*
das Stud*ium*	die Stud*ien*
das Mäd*chen*	die Mäd*chen*
das Fräu*lein*	die Fräu*lein*

Apart from these groups, there are no other neuter endings which follow any certain pattern, and a dictionary should always be consulted.

feminine nouns

1   This group is very reliable. Nouns having the following end-
    ings in the singular are always feminine:

    -ung   -ei   -in*   -heit   -keit
    -schaft   -ur   -ik   -ion   -ität

*When the feminine form of a masculine noun is made by adding
-in (der Freund, die Freundin), the plural form adds -nen (die
Freundinnen).

2   Short nouns ending in:

    -st   -cht   -ft   -t

    are mostly feminine and form their plural by adding an
    umlaut over the vowel (ä äu ö ü) and an -e or -en, but check
    for gender and plural in a dictionary.

Most feminine nouns in German have their plural ending in -n or
-en.

25 Weak masculine and adjectival nouns

1 Weak masculine nouns

There is a small but important group of nouns, all masculine,
which add -n or -en to every case in the singular except the
nominative and to all plural cases. These are known as *weak*
nouns, for example, *der Junge* (boy).

der Junge (boy)	Nominative	Accusative	Genitive	Dative
Singular	der Junge	den Jungen	des Jungen	dem Jungen
Plural	die Jungen	die Jungen	der Jungen	den Jungen

Other common nouns in this group are:

der Mensch (person)   der Matrose (sailor)
der Student (student)   der Soldat (soldier)
der Knabe (lad)   der Held (hero)

der Kamerad (friend)   der Löwe (lion)
der Neffe (nephew)   der Name (name; genitive des
der Polizist (policeman)   Namens)

Note particularly that *der Herr* (gentleman) takes *-n* in the singular but *-en* in all plural cases, as follows.

der Herr (the gentleman)	*Nominative*	*Accusative*	*Genitive*	*Dative*
Singular	der Herr	den Herrn	des Herrn	dem Herrn
Plural	die Herren	die Herren	der Herren	den Herren

2 Adjectival nouns

Another small group of nouns adds endings throughout the various cases as though they were in fact adjectives (see declension table, p 21). They begin with a capital letter and take *adjective* endings at the end of the noun for the appropriate case for example, *der Alte* (old man), *die Alte* (old woman).

der Alte die Alte	*Nominative*	*Accusative*	*Genitive*	*Dative*
Singular Masculine	der Alte ein Alter	den Alten einen Alten	des Alten eines Alten	dem Alten einem Alten
Singular Feminine	die Alte eine Alte	die Alte eine Alte	der Alten einer Alten	der Alten einer Alten
Plural	Plural adjectival nouns preceded by an article always end in *-en* in all cases, i.e. *die Alten* could be both 'the old men' or 'the old ladies', or 'the old people'.			

Other common adjectival nouns are:

der/die Arme   the poor man/woman
der/die Reiche   the rich man/woman
der/die Bekannte   the acquaintance
der/die Deutsche   the German
der/die Erwachsene   the grown-up

der/die Fremde	the stranger, foreigner
der/die Reisende	the traveller
der/die Verwandte	the relative
*der Beamte	the official

*Note that the feminine of *der Beamte* is *die Beamtin,* which is not an adjectival noun (see p 99, feminine nouns). Notice also that adjectival nouns generally refer to people and therefore only masculine and feminine forms are given.

26 Strong adjective endings

When an adjective and noun are used without an article, demonstrative word or possessive adjective (which usually show the case of the noun), the adjective must take what is called a strong ending to show case as shown in the examples below.

Guter Wein kostet viel Geld.
(Good wine is expensive)
Ich brauche heiß*es* Wasser.
(I need hot water)
Bei schön*em* Wetter, mit groß*er* Freude.
(In good weather; with great pleasure)

The full range of endings is shown below, set out in the same way as the declension table (p 21.) It can be seen that the strong adjective endings below correspond to the ending of *der das* and *die* in all cases except the genitive masculine and neuter singular.

	Nominative	Accusative	Genitive	Dative
Masc.	gut*er* Wein	gut*en* Wein	gut*en* Weins	gut*em* Wein
Neut.	gut*es* Bier	gut*es* Bier	gut*en* Biers	gut*em* Bier
Fem.	gut*e* Suppe	gut*e* Suppe	gut*er* Suppe	gut*er* Suppe
Plur.	gut*e* Speisen	gut*e* Speisen	gut*er* Speisen	gut*en* Speisen

27 Notes on phrases of time, manner, place

Word Order (see also position of the verb, p 67).

Phrases of time (saying when something happened)
              manner (saying how something happened)
              place (saying where something happened)
are always placed in the sentence in the order of:
time before manner before place (T.M.P.)

> Ich kam um zwei Uhr mit meinem Freund in der Schule an.
> (I arrived at school at two o'clock with my friend.)

Any one of these phrases may be omitted without affecting the order of the two remaining.

> Ich kam um zwei Uhr in der Schule an.
> (I arrived at school at two o'clock.)

Note: If one of these phrases is placed at the beginning of the sentence for emphasis, the remaining ones are still placed in the above order.

> In unserer Schule sollen die Kinder immer fleißig arbeiten.
> (In our school children are always supposed to work hard.)